One God

One God

The Deity revealed in Jesus

Peter Cotterell

First Published in 2006 by Spring Harvest Publishing Division and
Authentic Media

12 11 10 09 08 07 06   7 6 5 4 3 2 1

Authentic Media
9 Holdom Avenue, Bletchley, Milton Keynes, MK1 1QR, UK
and 129 Mobilization Drive, Waynesboro, GA 30830-4575, USA
www.authenticmedia.co.uk
Authentic Media is a division of Send the Light Ltd., a company
limited by guarantee (registered charity no. 270162)

British Library Cataloguing in Publication Data

A catalogue record for this book is available from
the British Library

ISBN 1-85078-685-2

Cover design by fourninezero design.
Print Management by Adare Carwin
Printed in Great Britain by Haynes, Sparkford, Yeovil, Somerset

ONE GOD CONTENTS

Is God the God of Jews only? Is he not the God of Gentiles too?
Yes, of Gentiles too, since there is only one God (Rom. 3:29-30).

1. Why we need God

The meaninglessness of life	1
The search for justice: it's not fair!	5
Rules to live by	9
Faith to die for	12
And after death?	15

2. What it is to be God

The three Omnis – Omnipresence: everywhere, or just with us?	18
Omniscience: well, at least he doesn't know what it is to sin	19
Omnipotence: well, he can't make me if I don't want to	21

3. Ideas about God

The Creator: But me . . . an insignificant speck in a vast universe	25

Someone who can do what I can't do:
   The importance of prayer   28
Books that tell me: Qur'an, Bhagavad Gita,
   an unwritten 'Bible'. *The* Bible   33
The Bible and other religions   35
A special problem: Islam   39
A special problem: the Trinity   42

4. Rejecting God
The huge problem of human suffering   46
God and my family   50
The huge growth of atheism   51

5. One God in many religions?
The three monos: Judaism, Islam and
   Christianity   54
Hinduism and Buddhism   73
The Traditional Religions   77
Allah, Yahweh, Krishna, Buddha, Waq   80
All right? All wrong? Only one right?   80
Six explanations of religions   81

6. Salvation: The crucial issue
Laws are no help   84
The two *ideas*   87
The eight *illustrations*   88
The Holy Spirit   97

7. Only one God
There can't be two creators   103
We can't have two sets of rules   104
Pluralist, inclusivist, exclusivist   106

How do we know the One God?
 How can we be sure?   111
A disappointment   114
 The Jews have not recognised their
  promised Messiah
 The Muslims have not met the real Jesus
'If only you knew' (Jn. 4:10)   117

Chapter One

Why we need God

The meaninglessness of life
The search for justice: it's not fair!
Rules to live by
Faith to die for
And after death?

The meaninglessness of life

Life isn't fair. How often have you said that? The problem is that bad things happen to good people and good things go on happening to bad people. We feel that it just isn't fair. Good people should be rewarded and bad people should be punished. Too often it's the other way round: poor people get exploited and rich people oppress them, but without anyone trying to bring in justice for the poor. The Preacher (Ecclesiastes) puts it very clearly:

> Again I looked and saw all the oppression that was taking place under the sun:
> I saw the tears of the oppressed –

And they have no comforter;
Power was on the side of their oppressors –
And they have no comforter (Eccl. 4:1).

The books of justice don't balance, but we feel that they should. Of course the books won't balance just because I want them to, but most people feel that they *should* balance. All we mean is that, in life, if I look at the bad things that happen to me, and assume that they are punishments for the bad things I've done, then the two ought to cancel each other out. Most of us don't expect much in the way of rewards for the good things we do (probably because we are more aware of the bad things we do) but when something hits us really hard, an accident, an illness, for example, all of us tend to ask: 'Why should this happen to me?'

Job faced this problem. Everything seemed to go wrong in his life: Arab raiders attacked his livestock out in the fields and carried off his donkeys and camels and oxen. Fire from heaven (lightning?) struck his flocks of sheep and killed them. A tornado hit the house where his children were eating a meal: the house collapsed on top of them and they all died. As if that was not enough, Job himself became ill with some massive infection. It produced sores all over his body, fever, unrelenting pain. It gave him nightmares, changed his very appearance and he lost weight. His friends came to comfort him, but were shocked at his appearance. Still, their theology had an explanation: he had sinned in some terrible way, and this was God's punishment for it. Probably up to this point Job had accepted this neat explanation of human suffering, but now he has to question it: he knows that he has not committed any sin that could justify such terrible punishment.

Perhaps we can modify the simple explanation of suffering: maybe the good things I've done might cancel out some of the bad things I've done so that I won't have quite so much punishment. That seems to lie behind the Muslim distinction between tithes (*zakat*), which must be paid over to the mosque and for which there is no reward, and philanthropy (*sadaqa*) for which there is a reward both now and at the time of judgement. One Muslim, al-Hasan al-Basri, said 'Whoever gives one dirham (penny) of sadaqa in Jerusalem (gifts given in holy cities are more valuable than gifts given anywhere else) gains his ransom from hellfire.' So according to Islam good deeds done now may not be rewarded now but will be rewarded later. But life *here and now* doesn't seem to work out the way we feel it should. Life isn't fair and it even seems pointless to try to live a 'good' life because there's no apparent reward for doing so. Life seems meaningless.

Many people were forced to think about this apparent meaninglessness of life, the unfairness of it all, and especially to think again about the idea of a compassionate God, when the Tsunami disaster hit the area around the Indian Ocean on December 26th 2004. An undersea earthquake produced a massive tidal wave that smashed into the surrounding coastlands, killing maybe a quarter of a million men, women and children.

After the disaster, the Indonesian columnist, author, and Muslim leader Emha Ainun Nadjib wrote an article for *Gatra* magazine. In his article the thousands of souls of the people of Aceh killed by the Tsunami torrents are confronted by seven spirits who develop a kind of antiphonal dialogue with them:

> 'Disaster is still disaster', says one of the figures, with a strange voice, its timbre like nothing ever heard before.
> 'Cruelty is still cruelty', says another of the beings.
> 'Injustice is still injustice', says yet another.

'Disaster because of whom? Whose cruelty? Whose injustice' Who do you mean?' asks one of the figures who appears to be a leader among them.

To their great shock, the thousands of souls hear, coming from all their mouths, the sudden unanimous voice, 'The Lord!'

'The Lord makes disaster? The Lord is cruel and unjust?'

The souls do not understand why, but yet again they respond in unison, 'Yes!'

'Is disaster, cruelty and injustice something that is created or something that creates? Are they created things or are they Creator?'

'Created things,' the souls respond, again in unison.

'Then if disaster, cruelty and injustice are created, who is their Creator?'

'The Lord.'

'So the Lord creates disaster and cruelty and injustice?'

'Yes.'

'I'm asking once more. So it is the Lord who creates disaster, cruelty and injustice?'

'Yes.'

'Just as he creates good fortune, good behaviour and understanding?'

'Yes.'

'Just as he created heaven, but also hell?'

'Yes.'

'As he created all of you, all humans, all animals, all the universe, heaven and earth, mountains and rivers, land and forest, and absolutely everything else; there is nothing that exists except what he created?'

'Yes.'

'Did the Lord create the universe, heaven and earth, and all of you by buying something, or borrowing the ingredients from another source – just as you prepare a meal by buying rice in the market?'

'No.'
'Was there any other who had a part in or made a con-
tribution to the Lord's making of all creatures?'
'No.'
'So in that man-making business, how many shares does
the Lord have?'
'One hundred percent.'[1]

So if we have an omnipotent God, he must be responsi-
ble for injustice. Allah is omnipotent, could have pre-
vented that Tsunami disaster, but didn't. And yet the
Qur'an repeatedly refers to Allah as 'The Merciful, the
Compassionate.' The Bible presents Yahweh as the God
who loves justice. But we don't see justice: life is not fair.
At least we would have to say that between the two
apparent boundaries of life and death life seems meaningless.

The search for justice: it's not fair!

'Justice' is one of the great words of the Old Testament,
the Bible of the Jewish people. Isaiah tells his people:

Stop doing wrong,
learn to do right!
Seek justice,
encourage the oppressed.
Defend the cause of the fatherless,
    plead the case of the widow (Is.1:16-17).

And so far as God himself is concerned he says:

---

[1] Emha Ainun Dajib, 'Aceh Accuses,' *Gatra,* 8 January 2005,
translated by A. Hasibuan (Ailish Eves).

> I, the Lord, love justice;
> I hate robbery and iniquity (Is. 61:8).

Perhaps the most famous of all the Bible's references to justice is in Amos 5:23-24:

> Away with the noise of your songs!
> I will not listen to the music of your harps.
> But let justice roll on like a river,
> righteousness like a never-failing stream!

The prophet Micah sings to the same tune:

> He has showed you, O man, what is good.
> And what does the Lord require of you?
> To act justly and to love mercy
> and to walk humbly with your God (Mich. 6:8).

But the Bible is not blind to the facts: life is not fair, and only too often we don't see justice rolling on like a river. In the collection of Proverbs one of the reasons why we don't get justice is explained:

> A poor man's field may produce abundant food,
> but injustice sweeps it away (Prov. 13:23).

At a first reading it may seem that Proverbs offers a typical capitalistic and elitist explanation of poverty. This is nicely illustrated by the references to 'the sluggard' in Proverbs. When he should be ploughing he isn't, and that explains his poverty (Prov. 20:4). He stays inside his house with some kind of excuse, however foolish: 'There is a lion outside!' (Prov. 22:13). He is in bed, yawning, stretching, when everyone else is out working (Prov. 26:14). He won't weed his fields and he won't repair his fences (Prov. 24:30-34). So that's the reason for his poverty: he is bone lazy.

But Proverbs makes it clear that the problem of poverty is not solved simply by blaming the poor. Poverty may come because a man is lazy or because he is exploited. Wealth and prosperity may come because a man works long and hard and is righteous, or it may come precisely because he is not righteous and exploits the poor. There are dishonest scales, lying tongues, ruthless men, cunning men, who store up their grain until the price rises, and the poor hate them for it (11:26).

But through it all there runs a single proposition: it is right to do what is right. There is a God who ultimately judges us all: 'the faithless will be fully repaid for their ways' (Prov. 14:14). Take God out of the equation and life is unfair; it doesn't make sense to try to do what is right. But put God in, accept the fact that he has laid down how we ought to live, recognise that death is not the end and that we must all have our lives judged . . . and then life takes on meaning, despite all the admitted unfairness.

And that is a reminder of the frustrations experienced by the farmers of the Third World: their crops are often good but the prices paid by the rest of the world are not. The search for justice demands that we look two ways if we want to explain the fact that too often it isn't there: to God, who says that he is a God of justice, but also to the people around us, who are only too ready to exploit the weak, the defenceless and even the hungry. We look to God, and we find expressed with devastating clarity in the Bible that he is a God of justice and that he demands that his people should be people of justice themselves, and should stand up for justice wherever there is injustice. So we then must look inwards, at ourselves, to ask whether we act justly, and we must look outwards to see what we can do to right the injustices by which we are surrounded.

In an attempt to ensure justice we have rules and we have laws. Everywhere we look there are rules: family rules ('If you can't eat your cabbage then you can't have any pudding'), work rules ('If you are off sick for more than three days you must produce a doctor's certificate') and the rules that govern the country ('You must pay income tax on your earnings.') But the rules don't seem to work very well: if I wait long enough I just might get my pudding even if I haven't eaten the hated cabbage, I think that I can cook up a doctor's certificate on my computer, and if I don't tell the government what I earn, they can't charge me income tax.

Almost every day we are aware of people breaking the rules and getting away with it. They may well be caught by the police, but then the charges are dismissed on some technicality. Again there is the problem that we never know the whole facts about any apparent crime. Sometimes it's just one person's word against another's, and then it's almost impossible to be sure that any decision taken is a just decision.

One haunting example of injustice is the case of the murder of a woman and her child in London in 1950. Their bodies had been buried in the garden of the house where she had lived with her husband, Timothy Evans. He was accused of murdering her. Their lodger, who lived in the downstairs flat in the same house, was one of the witnesses against him. Timothy Evans was found guilty of the murders and was executed, protesting his total innocence to the last. Three years later the lodger, John Christie, was arrested for multiple murders, and then was found guilty of the murder of the wife and child of Timothy Evans as well. In 1963, thirteen years after his execution, Timothy Evans was given a posthumous pardon. Where was justice?

Rules to live by

If you were the only person in the universe you wouldn't need any rules to live by. You could do exactly as you liked, when you liked and how you liked. But you aren't the only person in the universe. There are other people all around you. And there's God. Because there are other people around us we need rules that will enable us to get along peacefully. Because there is God we need rules that will tell us what we should do and what we should not do: rights and wrongs as he sees them. But here is a problem: people simply can't agree on what the rules ought to be. It's not even true that everyone believes that we should love one another. Plenty of people believe that we should love everyone who belongs to our nation or our clan or our tribe, or even just our family. Not everybody believes that we should love everybody. Nearly everyone of us finds it difficult to like (let alone love!) certain people: Americans, the Irish, Arabs, 'coloured' people (aren't we all coloured?): we call it prejudice and we all seem to suffer from it.

And then we have God. And he has *told* us what the rules are. Through Jesus we know how we ought to live.

Let's look again at this question of rules to live by. In 1948 the United Nations produced the Declaration of Universal Human Rights. Most countries signed up to it. Saudi Arabia did not, because the rights included the right to change your religion and Islam does not recognise that particular 'right'. Other Muslim countries did sign the Declaration, but in fact (often despite what was stated in their own national constitutions) continued to deny to Muslims the right to leave Islam. Now here's the difficulty for the UN: the authority for what the Saudis and other Muslims believe is quite clear: the Qur'an, which, they say, is God's revelation to humanity through

Muhammad. But where is the authority for the UN Declaration? There's no mention of God in it, so God is not the underlying authority. It is not a *universal* declaration since more than two billion Muslims don't agree with it, and that's almost exactly one fifth of the world's population. The Declaration, in reality, is the rather pious, optimistic, idealistic composition of a few, mainly western, politicians, produced just after the second world war. Times have changed. The composition of the United Nations has changed. A Declaration of Human Rights produced by today's United Nations would be very different from the one produced more than fifty years ago. If, in fact, they could agree on the wording of any Declaration.

But even apart from the UN Declaration we have disagreements about the rules to live by. When it comes to abortion, single-sex marriages, genetic engineering, the free market, paying interest on our borrowings, alcoholic drinks, freedom of speech, divorce, euthanasia . . . we don't all agree on the rules.

When it comes to real rules to live by we need someone to tell us what they are, someone we can trust, someone who knows. In fact we need God. But, and it's a big but, for most religions God is out there somewhere and we can't ask him about the rules. True enough some religions have a book with some rules in it. But Christianity has this enormous advantage: we have both a book and we have Jesus: God, who was born into this world, lived as a child in this world, worked in this world, died, was buried, came back to us from death, proving that he was who he said he was, and in doing all that showed us how the rules set out in the book could be worked out in life.

And yet . . . Jesus didn't deal in rules but in principles. Rules can be stifling, as anyone knows who has had to battle with the rules of the Inland Revenue people, or the rules relating to immigration. 'There are the rules: don't argue.' I went to visit an Ethiopian lady who was in hospital. She had phoned, asking me to go as she was seriously ill. So I went. I went to the receptionist at the hospital welcome desk and asked which ward the lady was in. 'Will you please tell me her home address?' I didn't know her home address. She had lived with my wife and me for a year, but I didn't know her home address now. 'All right, then, tell me her telephone number.' Well, she had phoned me, I hadn't phoned her, and I didn't know her telephone number. 'I'm sorry, but unless you know her address or her telephone number I can't tell you which ward she is in.' She was sorry . . . but that was in the rules. In this case, it was a particularly stupid rule. I had an apology from the hospital months later, but my Ethiopian friend (wherever she is) probably still thinks that I promised to go to see her but didn't go. I couldn't see her because of the rules: unkind, inflexible, inexorable.

On one occasion the Pharisees came to Jesus, bringing a woman to him for judgement . . . 'Teacher, this woman was caught in the act of adultery. In the Law, Moses commanded us to stone such women. Now what do you say?' (Jn. 8:4-5). No mention of what had happened to the man involved, just this frightened woman: *she* knew what the Law said. It was a simple case: a sin and its punishment set out in the Law, a woman caught by credible witnesses committing the sin. So the punishment, to be stoned to death, inexorably follows. Jesus had a different way of dealing with the problem. Probably today we would call it lateral thinking. The Law said that she was to be stoned. Then someone must throw the stones: 'If any one of you is without sin, let him be the first to throw a stone at her' (Jn. 8:7). There's the problem with

applying the Law: who is fit to apply it? As a bit of dog-
gerel verse, which has somehow stuck with me through
the years, has so concisely put it:

> There's so much good in the worst of us
> And so much bad in the best of us
> That it ill becomes any of us
> To talk about the rest of us.

Her accusers melted away. But Jesus didn't just excuse
the woman: 'Go now and leave your life of sin.'

Faith to die for

Being a Christian isn't always easy. It's a long time since
we had real widespread persecution of Christians in
Britain, but who knows what the future holds for us?

In very many parts of the world Christianity has to be
a faith to die for. In Indonesia, Malaysia, Pakistan,
Sudan, Nigeria and North Korea, to be a Christian is a
dangerous thing. The very fact that Christians have a
different set of rules, live by a different set of principles,
makes other people angry: they want us to be like them.

This is the basic idea lying behind that uncomfortable
word 'holy', used so often in both the Old Testament and
the New Testament. At its heart that word means 'different.' Holy pots and pans used in the Temple were different from other pots and pans, holy oil, used to anoint
the priests was different from other oil; the holy place in
the Temple was different from any other place, and holy
people were meant to be different from other people. But
society doesn't like people who are different. Sometimes
society tries to get rid of them, as the Nazis tried to get
rid of the Jews, as the Roman emperor Nero tried to get

rid of the Christians. In the past, when Christians had great political power, they were only too ready to persecute Jews, people who had different beliefs and different customs from their own.

When a great fire burned down a large part of Rome there were some who were ready to blame Nero for it. He blamed the Christians. Hundreds were arrested, some were tied to posts in Nero's garden, doused with pitch and used as torch-light for one of his parties. In the sixteenth century Muhammad the Left-Handed (Ahmad ibn Ibrahim) led a Muslim invasion of Ethiopia. Two local governors who were Christians were captured by Muhammad's followers and brought before him:

> He said, 'What is the matter with you that you haven't become Muslims when the whole country has Islamized?' They replied, 'We don't want to become Muslims.' He said, 'Our judgement on you is that your heads be cut off.' They said, 'Welcome.' The Imam was surprised at their reply and ordered them to be executed.[2]

There have been plenty of Christian martyrs in recent years. If David Barrett and Tod Johnson are right, there were 167,000 Christian martyrs in 2004![3]

Perhaps we should ask ourselves: is my faith, my belief in God, worth dying for? Is it that important?

Just one word of caution here: people will die for something that they believe to be true even though it

---

[2] J.S. Trimingham, *Islam in Ethiopia* (London: OUP, 1952), p88.

[3] 'Annual Statistical Table on Global Mission 2004', *International Bulletin of Missionary Research* 28, 1, January 2004.

might not be true. There have been Christian martyrs and Muslim martyrs and Hindu martyrs and Buddhist martyrs and Marxist martyrs, each one dying for their faith. So the fact that Christians have often laid down their lives for their faith doesn't prove that Christianity is the right religion. But still our faith should be something we are prepared to die for.

Why should our faith be that important? Religion deals with the present life, but it deals with something far more important: the life that comes after death. If there is something, anything, after death, it is important that we should have the right idea about it. Christianity insists that there is life after death, and also insists that there is judgement to be faced after death, a time when the apparent injustices of life here will be put right. But Christianity also deals in eternity. Where Hinduism talks about re-incarnation, coming back into this world as a reward or punishment for the way I live, Christianity says that death is simply the doorway between time and eternity. Seen like that, it is obviously vastly more important that I prepare for eternity than that I should hang on to time. As the hymn *Amazing Grace* reminds us about the nature of heaven:

> When we've been there ten thousand years,
> Bright shining as the sun,
> We've no less days to sing God's praise
> Than when we first begun.

Christians are encouraged to live each day now, bearing in mind eternity up there ahead of us. Yet again we are forced to ask the question: is Christianity right in what it says? Is the God of the Bible the One God? Is the teaching of Jesus just the teaching of one more religious teacher, or is it the One God, incarnate, here amongst us, telling us by his resurrection: there *is* life beyond this one, and there *is* a right way to live now, and the way I have lived *is* the way you should live.

And after death?

Between the two apparent boundaries of birth and death life seems to be meaningless. But what if one of those boundaries simply doesn't exist? In fact, all religions assume that beyond death life goes on. Hinduism, in fact, dissolves both boundaries: we exist before our latest 'birth' and we will go on existing after our next 'death'. The Traditional Religions (for example the religions of Africa before either Christianity or Islam arrived) believe that life goes on. Very often they will bury with the dead the sort of things they might need in the next world: cooking pots, a pipe to smoke, a hunting knife. The Egyptians believed that the dead needed in the next life everything they had needed in the present life:

> a substantial dwelling, food and drink, as well as servants, slaves and officials . . . . But above all considerations the body itself had to be ensured against every destructive influence, to enable the freely wandering soul – ka in Egyptian – to find its way back to where it belonged.'[4]

Hence the pyramids, provided for the dead pharaohs, the careful preservation of the bodies, the lavish use of gold in their tombs.

---

[4] C.W. Ceram, *Gods, Graves and Scholars* (Harmondsworth: Penguin, 1951), p159.

Christianity adds one thing that the Traditional Religions hardly ever have: judgement. That's what makes some kind of sense of an otherwise apparently meaningless life: a judgement from God who knows all the facts, who alone can produce real justice.

The Christian view of what happens after death is not all judgement, doom and gloom. On the contrary, once we believe in God, once we recognize his rules, once we see beyond death, we can see a glorious heaven, so wonderful, in fact, that even John, who was allowed a vision of it, was unable really to find words to describe it all . . . streets paved with gold, a tree that kept on giving fruit, twelve different kinds, right through the year, leaves that could heal. I don't suppose that we should take it all too literally: gold would be uncomfortable to walk on, and blinding in the light of God's glory. But we get the idea. Bede, in his history of early Christianity in England, tells how it was that this new religion, Christianity, was allowed to be preached. Edwin of Northumbria was discussing the question with his advisers. One of them used an interesting illustration.

> Life is like this. It's as if you, the King, are sitting in the great banqueting hall with your counsellors, enjoying a feast. The hall is peaceful, warm. Outside a storm is raging, it is cold, snowing, inhospitable. And then a bird flies in through one of the windows . . . flutters about, and then out again through another window. That's a picture of life. We are born, we live in comfort, just for a few years, but then we must die, like that bird we must go out into that inhospitable world, the world beyond death. And if anyone can tell us about that other world . . . we should hear him.

It's a fascinating insight into what people were thinking, and still are thinking, about life after death. Christianity has a different picture from that of the Traditional Religions, a different picture from that of most people: *the storm is inside the banqueting hall!*

If there is such a 'place' as heaven then we need to know how to get there. As we shall see in chapter five, Christians say that it is through faith in Jesus as Saviour that we can gain heaven (and, of course, live as we are supposed to live here and now). Islam says that it's a matter of obedience to rules, the balance of good deeds and bad deeds. At the judgement, the recording angels give everybody the record of their lives, each life set out in a book. The book is received in the left hand if the bad deeds outweigh the good deeds, but in the right hand if the good deeds outweigh the bad deeds. One very popular sect of the Buddhist religion, New Land Buddhists, say that the paradise of the New Land is promised to anyone who calls on the name of Amida-Buddha. Jews say that Gentiles must obey the seven laws given to Noah. Hindus say that there is no heaven to go to. It doesn't seem that these religions are speaking with one voice. . .

Chapter two

What it is to be God

The three omnis
*   Omnipresence: everywhere, or just with us?*
*   Omniscience: well, at least he doesn't know what it is to sin*
*   Omnipotence: well, he can't* make *me if I don't want to*

Somehow these three words seem to have crept into our belief about God: he is everywhere, omnipresent, he knows everything, he is omniscient, and he can do anything, he is omnipotent.

The three Omnis – Omnipresence: everywhere, or just with us?

The first one isn't too difficult. The psalmist settled the matter:

> Where can I go from your Spirit?
> Where can I flee from your presence?
> If I go up to the heavens, you are there;
> if I make my bed in the depths, you are there.
> If I rise on the wings of the dawn,

if I settle on the far side of the sea,
even there your hand will guide me,
your right hand will hold me fast.
If I say, 'Surely the darkness will hide me,
and the light become night around me,'
even the darkness will not be dark to you . . .
(Ps. 139:7-12).

So God is everywhere.

That doesn't mean that everything you see is in some sense 'God.' It just means that he can't be shut out from anything we do or anywhere we go. And that 'we' means everybody. The Syrian army commander, Naaman, was cured of his leprosy by Elisha. His response was to profess some kind of conversion: he would become a worshipper of Yahweh. But how could he do that in Syria? God was the God of Israel and only operated in Israel. Answer: take Israel with you: two loads of soil carried on the backs of a pair of mules should be sufficient: then he would have Israel in Syria, and God would be there for him (2 Kgs. 5:1-19).

But God is everywhere, for everyone. His character is compassion, for rich, for poor, for hungry, for thirsty, for young, for old, for the educated, for the ignorant. He knows us all, cares for us all, and, as Joel put it and as Peter repeated it: 'Everyone who calls on the name of the Lord will be saved' (Joel 2:32, Acts 2:21).

Omniscience: well, at least he doesn't know what it is to sin

What about the second omni, Omniscience? This is obviously a more difficult issue: we can see at once a few of the things God can't know. Most importantly Jesus never sinned, and so is unable actually to know what it is to be a sinner. Jesus became sin for us, but he didn't become a sinner for us.

It's as well to remember that when Jesus became man he temporarily laid aside his omniscience. When he was a child he didn't know everything, though he knew enough to ask the theologians of his day some obviously difficult questions (Lk. 2:43-47). But then I've found that it's the questions that children ask that are the most difficult to answer, not the questions of the theologians: Christian parents will sympathise. But in case we're tempted to think that Jesus, being God incarnate, always knew everything let us remember what Luke wrote: 'Jesus grew in wisdom and stature' (Lk. 2:52).

Jesus knew more than other people knew: many people believed simply because of the miracles he performed. But 'Jesus would not entrust himself to them, for he knew all men. He did not need man's testimony about man, for he knew what was in a man' (Jn. 2:24-5). Psalm 139 confirms this wonderful and yet rather frightening fact:

> O LORD, you have searched me
> and you know me.
> You know when I sit and when I rise;
> you perceive my thoughts from afar.
> You discern my going out and my lying down;
> you are familiar with all my ways.
> Before a word is on my tongue
> you know it completely, O LORD (Ps. 139:1-4).

It has to be like that, because of the judgement we are one day to face: how could even God judge fairly, justly, unless he knew everything about us: not only what we have done, but also what we have thought, what we have wanted to do, what effect our childhood experiences might have had on our later behaviour?

Omnipotence: well, he can't make me if I don't want to

God can't do the logically impossible. He can't produce a circle with corners to it, or make five plus five equal nine. More seriously, he can't do *anything* that is contrary to his nature. He can't be unjust, for example. But that seems to mean that he can't simply shut his eyes to our sin. Paul gets it absolutely right in his letter to the church at Rome:

> God presented him [Jesus] as a sacrifice of atonement, through faith in his blood. He did this to demonstrate his justice, because in his forbearance he had left the sins committed beforehand [before the death of Jesus] unpunished – he did it to demonstrate his justice at the present time, so as to be just and the one who justifies those who have faith in Jesus (Rom. 3:25-26).

It is enormously important to realise that God can't *make* me do anything if I don't want to. He has given us freedom to choose how we will live (otherwise what's the point of all those verses of the Bible that command us to choose?) He can't make me good, any more than I can *make* my daughters love me. I can go a long way in making them obey me, but I can't make them love me. God can tell us how we ought to live (and he did that when he became incarnate, when Jesus came here), and he can make it possible for us to live the right way (and he did that when he sent his Holy Spirit), but he can't make us do what we don't ourselves *will* to do.

Here is one great difference between Christianity and Islam. Muslims believe that Allah has the whole history of the world planned out, from the biggest events to the smallest. He planned the Tsunami disaster. One Muslim leader said that it was to punish the pleasure-loving American holiday-makers: but of the 230,000 people who died only a tiny fraction were American holiday-makers: thousands were Indonesian and Thai children. Why were they singled out by Allah to die in a disaster intended to punish Americans? According to Islam, Allah has planned your life and your duty is to submit to that plan. Actually that's the basic meaning of 'Islam': (submission) submission to the plans of Allah.

Not all Muslims believe that Allah has planned every-thing. Some of the early Muslim philosophers and theologians (the 'Mutazilites') saw that if he has, then he can hardly blame us for our actions and there can't be a day of judgement. But most Muslims still believe in the idea of total predestination and that's why Muslims so often say 'Insha Allah', 'If Allah wills.' 'Will you be going to school tomorrow?' 'I will go to school tomorrow if Allah wills.' 'Will the window cleaner come today?' 'The window cleaner will come today if Allah wills.'

Unfortunately a good many Christians believe that God has planned everything. And that seems to be all right until something horrible happens: personal things like a car accident, a cot death, sudden illness, and the bigger things like the Tsunami or Auschwitz. Did God plan those things? The Muslim answer is 'Yes, Allah did.' The Christian answer is, 'No, Yahweh didn't.'

But. It is true that we should be careful about making our plans. James said:

> Now listen, you who say, 'Today or tomorrow we will go to this or that city, spend a year there, carry on business

and make money.' Why, you do not even know what will happen tomorrow . . . Instead, you ought to say, 'If it is the Lord's will, we will live and do this or that' (Jas. 4:13-15).

Christians should be aware that the only breath we have is the one we've got. The only day we have is today. We simply don't know about tomorrow, except that we know that God will be with us, just as he is with us today.

James was writing to Christians. But there are the millions of people out there who aren't Christians, who aren't inside God's kingdom, who do think that they are free to plan the future, who have no idea of a judgement that's coming. In fact this is one of the big differences between Christianity and Islam. Jesus told us that there is a Second Kingdom. Once he was accused of being in league with that kingdom and healing people through the power of Beelzebub, 'Lord of the Flies', a deliberate corruption of 'Beelzebul', 'Prince Baal', the name the Jews gave to Satan. He didn't deny that the Second Kingdom exists, but this is what he said:

> '*Every kingdom* divided against itself will be ruined, and every city or household divided against itself will not stand. If Satan drives out Satan, he is divided against himself. How then can *his kingdom* stand? And if I drive out demons by Beelzebub, by whom do your people drive them out? So then, they will be your judges. But if I drive out demons by the Spirit of God, then the *Kingdom of God* has come upon you' (Mt. 12:25-28: italics mine).

Every Kingdom . . . his kingdom . . . the Kingdom of God. Muslims believe in the existence of Satan but they don't believe in a Satanic *Kingdom*. Everything that happens is decreed by Allah. This is really important: for Christians there are two kingdoms and we are all in the one kingdom or the other. Of course we don't believe in the Satan that's usually seen in picture books, with red tights, horns and a pitchfork. But we do believe in evil, we know that it's there and we know that it doesn't come from God. There is a second kingdom at work.

God's kingdom hasn't come yet. That's why in the Lord's Prayer we pray 'Thy Kingdom come, Thy will be done, on earth as it is in heaven.' God's will *is* done in heaven and it *is* sometimes done on earth but we are all free to decide whether we will do his will or simply follow what we want to do.

So in one sense God is not omnipotent. He can't *make* me good. What he can do and what he has done is to take me out of that second kingdom, bring me into his Kingdom, and there make it possible for me to be good.

And here, once again, we have to choose between religions, between theologies, between theories, the Christian one and the Muslim one, between what Allah says and what Yahweh says; between Hindu ideas of right and wrong and Christian ideas; between the ethics of the Traditional Religions and the ethics of Christianity. There is just one right way because there is only one God.

Chapter three

Ideas about God

The Creator
  But me…an insignificant speck in a vast universe
Someone who can do what I can't do
  The importance of prayer
Books that tell me; Qur'an, Bhagavad Gita, An
  unwritten 'Bible'. The Bible
The Bible and other religions
A special problem: Islam
A special problem: the Trinity

The Creator: But me . . . an insignificant speck in a vast universe

Hinduism does not believe that the world had a beginning, nor that the world will have an end. It comes and goes, it dies and is born again, in an endless cycle of new creations. The Traditional Religions are interesting because they often have lower deities, lesser deities, but somewhere in the background there is the Creator. Usually the Traditional Religions don't have too much to do with this Creator: he is much too important, and much too far away.

But Christianity, Judaism and Islam join together in believing that God created this world, and in fact he created this universe and any other universes that might exist.

I am one person in a world population of six billion. To myself, to my family and friends, I may seem important. As one amongst six billion I am nothing. I stand on a whirling planet, just one of several planets, circling around a sun. If I go outside at night and look up I can see that broad band of light (popularly labelled the Milky Way because it looks as though someone up there has spilled a trail of milk across the heavens), which is made up of millions of other suns with their planets, making up my galaxy. In that immensity I am doubly, trebly, unimportant. But my galaxy in turn is just one of millions of galaxies, some larger, some smaller but reaching out into black holes beyond which is unimaginable immensity. And standing in some unimaginably tiny, insignificant corner of this universe I try to understand who the One God who created it all might be.

To drive home the absurdity of my search for meaning, let me put in some numbers. This earth is a tiny planet circling around the sun, and in its turn is circled by a moon. It is merely one of nine planets known to be circling the sun, and is by no means the largest of them. But that is only one almost trivial indication of the comparative insignificance of our world. Our sun is merely one of millions (say one hundred thousand million) in our galaxy, and the galaxy merely one amongst the millions (again say one hundred thousand million) in the universe. It is of less significance than one grain of sand amongst all the grains of sand on all the beaches of all the world. And I am one of six million people living on that one grain of sand!

However, the fact is that I am here, and I am trying to understand God. And this is because when God created the universe, he so designed it that we would one day appear in it and be able to live in it and, eventually, to ask questions about him. The universe is what the scientists call *anthropic*, designed for human beings. That doesn't mean that scientists all believe that God created the universe for us, or even that he created it at all. What they do believe is that for some reason this universe is peculiarly designed through its myriad laws in such a way that humanity would eventually appear.

John Polkinghorne, once a Professor of Mathematical Physics in the University of Cambridge, now retired and an Anglican minister, explains that:

> our universe represents a very tiny fertile patch in what is otherwise a desert area of possibility. For the development of fruitful complexity one needs: the right laws (neither so rigid that nothing really new can happen, nor so floppy that only chaos can ensue – quantum mechanics seems ideal from this point of view); the right kind of constituents (a universe consisting just of electrons and photons would not have a rich enough potential for varied structure); the right force strengths (e.g. nuclear forces able to generate the elements inside stars); and the right circumstances (e.g. a big enough universe). The Anthropic Principle is widely accepted in this scientific sense. There is greater variety of opinion about what wider significance might or might not be attached to that conclusion.[5]

Polkinghorne goes on to explain that in the early universe there were (amongst others) two opposing forces,

---

[5] John Polkinghorne, *Science and Theology* (London: SPCK, 1998), p37.

the force of expansion, driving matter apart, and the force of gravity, pulling matter together: 'At a very early epoch these two competing effects . . . were so closely balanced that they differed from each other by just one part in 10^{60}.'

He goes on to illustrate the statistic: 'If I took a target an inch wide and placed it on the other side of the observable universe, eighteen thousand million light years away, and took aim and hit the target, then I would have attained an accuracy of one in 10^{60}.'[6] But this incredible balance is necessary if on the one hand stars are to form and on the other hand the entire universe is not simply to collapse back in on itself before anything interesting could emerge from it.

What was interesting and what emerged from it was you, and me, and all humanity. And yet you are and I am just tiny specks in this vast universe. But we have something that nothing else in the universe has got: the ability to know God our Maker. We can know him because he determined that we should be able to know him. We can know him because in the act of creation he built into the universe the Incarnation: that he himself would come here, to this tiny insignificant speck, to show us the Father behind it all, and do it through the Son.

Someone who can do what I can't do: the importance of prayer

We can talk. We have this extraordinary gift of language. Creatures like birds and porpoises and lions and even

---

[6] 'God as Creator' in Robin Gill (ed.), *Readings in Modern Theology* (London: SPCK, 1995), p32.

rabbits can produce noises, but nowhere in the rest of our world is there anything else remotely as powerful as human language. It is the gift of language that makes science possible: scientists think to themselves, talk to others, write books about their thoughts and it all depends on language. Using language we can ask questions, give instructions, share experiences, talk about everyday events, express our love. And we can talk about the hard things of life, share our sorrows, express our doubts, and that helps, even if the people we are talking to can't do much about our problems or our sorrows.

But there is something called prayer. Islam ought not to have any *intercessory* prayer, because God has already fixed the future. The Muslim *salat*, 'prayer', is primarily concerned with giving glory to Allah. However, there is a place for an appeal to Allah, *Du'a*. To be effective an appeal to God should be made only if the one praying is ritually clean: has not eaten any forbidden food (such as pork), and has observed the rules about washing before prayer. One should pray at the right time, preferably during one of the five set times for *salat*. It is best to face towards Mecca and to raise the hands. As one writer explains, 'These conditions and rules for *du'a* are intended to surround it with guarantees of efficacy.'[7] Actually *du'a* does not always get the response from Allah that is hoped for, and that is why Folk Islam, what ordinary Muslims believe and do, has grown up alongside orthodox Islam. Muslims who are in trouble will usually go to someone who has a reputation for getting answers to prayer, rather than trusting to their own *du'a*. Very often

---

[7] From the article 'Du'a' in volume 2 of the *Encyclopaedia of Islam*, edited by B. Lewis, C. Pellat and J. Schacht (Leiden: Brill, 1965).

they will approach Allah through a Muslim saint, perhaps someone who died a long time ago but who was renowned for his holiness.

Sadly, for a good many Christians, prayer is simply a shopping list which we take to God. He is a kind of celestial supermarket, with the emphasis on the word 'super'. He has everything in stock, everything available, including such commodities as happiness. The Christian has only to ask. Unfortunately it doesn't seem to work. So when it doesn't seem to work we remember that we have to pray *'in the name of Jesus'*, so we pray again, tacking on the magic phrase 'and this we ask *in the name of Jesus.'* And if that doesn't work then we try reminding God about this magical formula, 'And this we ask in the *strong name* of Jesus.' And if that doesn't work then we remember that the Bible talks about two or three of us asking, so we get others to ask for what we are asking. And if that doesn't work then we can enrol a few hundred people, a few thousand people, and then surely God will have to give us what we are asking for. But still he can't be made to do what we want him to do. Too often our requests are selfish, thoughtless and with little idea of what God might expect of us: and then, inevitably, he doesn't do what we are demanding.

Asking 'in the name of Jesus' doesn't simply mean tacking the phrase 'and this we ask in the name of Jesus' on to the end of our prayers. Jesus once said that if we give someone a drink of water 'in my name' then we will be rewarded. But obviously he didn't mean that when we give someone a glass of water we should say 'In the name of Jesus!' What he meant was that we should give it as Jesus would have given it if he had been there. He would have not just given the glass of water: surely he would have taken time to stop and talk to the thirsty person. Applying that idea to today, when we give one of our homeless beggars some money we should do it 'in the name of Jesus', and stop to talk to them, be interested in them as real people loved by God. Now going back to praying 'in the name of Jesus' that means praying as Jesus would pray, and that would be praying, *knowing what God's will is*. And that also means admitting sometimes that just at this moment I don't really know what his will is . . . I'm too upset, too involved, too tired. And then it's right to pray 'if it is possible' or 'not my will, but your will be done.'

Prayer isn't telling God what to do: it's talking to him about what I'm doing, about what's happening, and asking him to show me what it is he is doing, and what it is he wants me to do in this difficult situation that I'm in. Prayer is thanking God for what he has done. Prayer is praising God for who he is. Prayer is confessing what I've done that I shouldn't have done. It's much more than a shopping list.

But why is it that so often our requests are turned down? Well, let's go back to creation. When God created the universe he made it an anthropic universe, the kind of universe in one corner of which I could live. But he had decided also that I would be free to choose. Those of us who are inside his kingdom want to choose what he wants. But there are millions outside the kingdom who don't particularly bother about what God wants. And God can't make them do what he wants. Too often their free will gets in the way of our prayers. We can certainly pray that a Christian will drive carefully and safely, and because the Christian driver is inside the Kingdom, God can, through the Holy Spirit, prompt them to drive carefully. But there are other drivers on the road, selfish, careless, godless drivers. Some of them have had a quick drink before starting out, some have just had a row with their husbands, some have just bought a new fast car and want to show off its power, and God can't take away their free will. Accidents happen even to careful and prayerful Christian drivers.

So is there no 'asking' prayer in Christianity? Of course there is, but obviously we should only ask for what God wills. Put the other way round, it's no good asking for anything that is contrary to God's will. We are not trying to twist God's arm so that he does what we want; rather we are trying to find out what he wants so that we can bring our plans into line with his. And here we have to remember that bad things happen to good people, that Christians are sometimes ill, are sometimes involved in accidents, and we all have to die.

So before we start asking God we need to ask ourselves: is this what God wants, or is it something that I want? John put it very clearly:

> This is the confidence we have in approaching God: that if we ask anything *according to his will*, he hears us. And if we know that he hears us – whatever we ask – we know that we have what we have asked of him (1 Jn. 5:14-15, italics mine).

Again this search to know God's will and then to ask for that is exactly in line with the Lord's Prayer:

> Our Father in heaven,
> hallowed be your name,
> your kingdom come,
> *your will be done*
> *on earth* as it is in heaven (Mt. 6:9-10, italics mine).

And very movingly it is exactly how Jesus prayed when he was confronted by the cross:

My Father, if it is possible, may this cup be taken from me. Yet not as I will, but as you will (Mt. 26:39).

Books that tell me: Qur'an, Bhagavad Gita, An Unwritten 'Bible'. *The* Bible

Write it down! Conversations are soon forgotten or else are misremembered. Anything important soon gets written down. All over the world there are inscriptions, carved into rocks, written on skins or papyrus or paper. There's the amazing copper scroll of Isaiah found amongst the Dead Sea Scrolls. There are the records of thousands of lives filed away in the Public Record Office: birth certificates, death certificates, marriage certificates, wills. Things that are important eventually get written down.

This is especially true of religious things. The Jewish people carefully recorded their own history and guarded that record with great care: the Jewish Bible. Hinduism has a massive literature, the Vedas (the word itself means 'knowledge') and there's the great Hindu classic, the Bhagavad Gita, 'The Song of God', which sets out one response to the problem of human suffering ('suffering is a myth'). There's the Qur'an, written in Arabic, the sacred book of Islam. Then there is a huge oral literature, carefully preserved from generation to generation of people who have not so far reduced their languages to writing, the literature of the Traditional Religions, what might be called an unwritten bible, the authoritative but unwritten books of the Traditional Religions. And there's the Christian Bible, Old Testament plus New Testament.

Each of these books seeks to tell the reader something about this world: how it began, where humanity came from, and how we ought to live. Often the books provide some description of life after death. Almost always there's an attempt to explain human suffering.

But yet again we are confronted by this problem: they don't agree with one another. They could all be wrong, one of them could be right, but it is not possible for the thinking person to say that *really* they are all saying the same thing. We have to choose.

Take the Bhagavad Gita and the answer it gives to the problem of suffering. Arjuna is a young prince, riding in his chariot between two opposing armies prepared to engage in a battle. It's a civil war: he has his own people on both sides. Arjuna imagines the carnage and recoils from it. The Lord Krishna explains the reality to him:

> Why grieve for those for whom no grief is due?. . . There was never a time when I was not, nor thou, nor these princes were not: there will never be a time when we shall cease to be . . . Those external relations which bring cold and heat, pain and happiness, they come and go; they are not permanent. Endure them bravely, O Prince. The hero whose soul is unmoved by circumstance, who accepts pleasure and pain with equanimity, only he is fit for immortality . . . The spirit kills not, nor is It killed . . . weapons cleave It not, fire burns It not, water drenches It not, and wind dries It not.[8]

The Song ends with the battle in which both armies are virtually destroyed.

Islam has its own holy book, the Qur'an, but adds to it various collections of traditions about the life of

---

[8] There are many versions of the Bhagavad Gita. This quote is taken from the beautifully illustrated version translated by Shri Purohit Swami (London: Faber and Faber, 1978), p15.

Muhammad; the Hadith. These two form the basis for Muslim beliefs and Muslim behaviour. One part of Sura ('chapter') 4 of the Qur'an deals with the crucifixion of Jesus. The passage says of the Jews that:

> They rejected faith; that they uttered against Mary a grave false charge;
> That they said (in boast), 'We killed Christ Jesus the son of Mary,
> The Messenger of Allah' –
> But they killed him not, nor crucified him,
> But so it was made to appear to them,
> And those who differ therein are full of doubts,
> With no certain knowledge, but only conjecture to follow,
> For of a certainty they killed him not . . .
>
> (*Qur'an Sura 4:* 156-157)

So the Qur'an says that Jesus was not crucified, and so no Muslim believes that Jesus died on the cross. But the New Testament has as its focus the death and resurrection of Jesus, atoning for the sins of the world. Now this is not a matter of theology or philosophy: it is a matter of history. Either Jesus *did* die on the cross (and the Bible is right), or else he did *not* die on the cross (and the Qur'an is right.).Even in today's so-called post-modern world we can't have two histories; both books can't be right. And then we have to add that both religions can't be right: it's one or the other, or neither, but not both. It's Allah or it's Yahweh, but not both.

The Bible and other religions

The absolute and exclusive claims of Yahweh are set out in Exodus 20:

You shall have no other gods before me.
You shall not make for yourself an idol in the form of anything in heaven above or on the earth beneath or in the waters below. You shall not bow down to them or worship them (Ex. 20:3-4).

The Old Testament writers frequently mock the gods of other religions. In Egypt Moses and his brother Aaron are pitched against the Egyptian magicians by Pharaoh. Aaron throws his staff down on the ground, and miraculously it becomes a snake. The Egyptian magicians can play that game: they throw down their sticks and their sticks become snakes . . . but then Aaron's snake swallows up the snakes of the magicians (Ex. 7:8-13). In Genesis we have the droll picture of Jacob's wife Rachel sitting on her father Laban's household idols (Gen. 31:33-35). Isaiah dismisses Bel and Nebo, idols of the Babylonians, because they can't even save themselves, still less those who worship them: they all go off to captivity together, the idols lashed on to the backs of donkeys (Is. 46:1-2). Perhaps the most telling of all the Old Testament passages is Isaiah 44:12-17:

The blacksmith takes a tool
and works with it in the coals;
he shapes an idol with hammers,
he forges it with the might of his arm.
He gets hungry and loses his strength;
he drinks no water and grows faint.

The carpenter measures with a line
and makes an outline with a marker;
he roughs it out with chisels
and marks it with compasses.
He shapes it in the form of man,

of man in all his glory,
that it may dwell in a shrine.

He cut down cedars,
or perhaps took a cypress or oak.
He let it grow among the trees of the forest,
or planted a pine, and the rain made it grow.

It is man's fuel for burning;
some of it he takes and warms himself,
he kindles a fire and bakes bread.
But he also fashions a god and worships it;
he makes an idol and bows down to it.

Half of the wood he burns in the fire;
over it he prepares his meal,
he roasts his meat and eats his fill.
He also warms himself and says,
'Ah! I am warm; I see the fire.'

From the rest he makes a god, his idol;
 he bows down to it and worships.
He prays to it and says,
 'Save me; you are my god.'

Elijah was quite prepared to take on Baal, one of the
gods of the Canaanite religion, adopted by many of the
Israelites of his day. A challenge: who can produce the
flame that will light the wood piled under the animals
that were to be offered up, one to Baal, another to
Yahweh? Baal's followers go first, and despite all their
shouting and dancing with no success: Baal is silent.
Says Elijah, 'Shout louder! Surely he is a god! Perhaps he
is deep in thought, or busy, or travelling. Maybe he is
sleeping and must be awakened!' (1 Kgs. 18:27). And

Elijah makes it clear: choose! 'How long will you waver between two opinions? If the Lord is God, follow him; but if Baal is God, follow him.' There's only one God.

In the New Testament, Paul's approach to the religions of his day is made clear by the craftsmen of Ephesus, who made their living by making silver shrines for the worshippers of Artemis. These shrines were copies of the enormous temple dedicated to the female goddess, whose statue in the temple was supposed to have dropped down from the sky. They accused him: 'He says that man-made gods are no gods at all' (Acts 19:23-27). It is interesting that later on when he wrote to the Christians at Ephesus, Paul confirmed what the craftsmen had said. He reminded the Christians that 'you were separate from Christ, excluded from citizenship in Israel and foreigners to the covenants of the promise, without hope and without God in the world' (Eph. 2:12).

Those two words 'without God' represent the one Greek word *atheoi*, from which we get our English word 'atheist'. Not that the Ephesians were atheists in our modern sense, people who don't believe in God, but atheists in Paul's sense: they had a god (Artemis), but they didn't have God (Yahweh).

The positive description of God (who he is, rather than who he isn't) is set out in Paul's letter to the church at Ephesus. He writes:

> There is one body and one Spirit – just as you were called to one hope when you were called – one Lord, one faith, one baptism, one God and Father of all, who is over all and through all and in all (Eph. 4:4-6).

That word 'one' hammers away any idea of many gods or even any idea of a divided Christianity. There is only one God, and he is Father, Son and Spirit. Consequently there is only one Christianity, marked by the future hope of glory, by its confession of Christ, by its one faith and by its practice of baptism.

This unity was there in the early church, and we might be inclined today to look around us at the church, carved up into hundreds of competing parties, and wonder where that 'one' has gone. But it hasn't gone. Despite what the 'one-and-onlys' might say, there is only one body of Christ: Catholic, Orthodox, Protestant, Charismatic, this whole bewildering kaleidoscope of beliefs and practices still boils down to the simple affirmation: one church. There is a heart to Christianity, a core, and to that core from time to time Christians go on adding, assuming that they are producing the *real* core, a core that produces *real* Christians and identifies the also-rans, the pseudo Christians. But whether it's the Mass, or speaking in tongues, or apostolic succession, or the King James Bible, nothing can alter Paul's assertion that we are one. Not all in one denomination, but all in one body. Just who is in that one body is not for us to say, still less who is *not* in that one body.

A special problem: Islam

The very heart of Islam is the belief in one God. The doctrine is called the doctrine of *tawhid*. The word is related to the Arabic word for one, *wahed*. Every time a Muslim says his *salat*, his ritual prayers, he repeats the basic confession of Muslim faith: 'There is no god but Allah, and Muhammad is his messenger.' There is the well known story of a slave named Bilal, who became a follower of Muhammad. He grasped that one fundamental teaching of Muhammad, that God is one, and he used to go around saying 'One! One!' That eventually annoyed his master: after all, the Arab people at that time worshipped hundreds of gods; their idols were stored in Mecca in the Ka'ba and that brought good trade to the Meccans as the Arabs from all around came in to worship their particular idol. One God? He ordered Bilal to stop. Bilal wouldn't: 'One! One!' So his master had him pegged out in the desert, a stone on his chest, without water, left there until he gave up his 'One! One!' But all Bilal said was 'One!' Fortunately for him, Abu Bekr, another Muslim but a well-to-do free man, came along, saw him, and offered to give Bilal's master another slave in exchange for Bilal. And then Abu Bekr set Bilal free.

So, Muslims worship one God, the Creator, and Christians worship one God, the Creator. Therefore Christians and Muslims worship the same God? Many Christians would answer yes. I am more cautious. The problem lies in that word 'God'. We use it in two ways, as meaning the God of our Bible, but also as the gods of other religions. A capital 'G' God and a small 'g' god. And we tend to switch from one to the other without noticing what we are doing. So let me be more precise: The Muslims worship one God, the Creator, Allah, and the Christians worship one God, the Creator, Yahweh. Is Allah the same as Yahweh?

This name Yahweh is the correct Hebrew name for the One God of the Bible. It used to be translated 'Jehovah' but that was a mistake and the mistake was made because Jews felt that God's name was too holy to pronounce. They couldn't alter the actual text of the Bible. Instead they added to the *consonants* of *Yahweh* the vowels of *adonai*, 'Lord', to produce Y-e-H-o-V-a, a word that is impossible in Hebrew. The impossible word reminded any Jewish reader to substitute *adonai* for the unutterable *Yahweh*. But Yehovah (or 'Jehovah') is quite possible in

English, so it was adopted as the name of God in the Old Testament.

So, once again, is Yahweh the same as Allah? Or is Yahweh the same as Krishna? Or is Yahweh the same as Buddha? Or is Yahweh the same as Waq, the god of many East African Traditional Religions?

Let's imagine that I have just bought a table. I visit a friend's house and find that he has a table. Has he got my table? Are they one and the same table? 'My table had four legs.' 'Mine only has three!' 'Ah, but looked at from a certain angle you can only see three of the legs of my table.' My table was green.' 'But my table is yellow!' 'Ah, but if you change the colour of the lighting the colour of the table will change, so maybe you have got my table.' 'My table was square.' 'But my table is round!' 'Ah, but if you look at it sideways on you can't see whether it's round or square, so maybe you have got my table.' 'No! A three-legged, yellow, round table is not the same as a four-legged, green, square table. I haven't got your table.'

Now look at this question of whether the gods of the different religions are all the same. We answer the question by describing each 'god' and comparing the results. One good biblical definition of Yahweh is that He is 'the God and Father of our Lord Jesus Christ' (Eph. 1:3). So is He the same as Allah? The fact is that the Qur'an condemns Christians because of their belief in the Trinity:

> They do blaspheme who say: Allah is one of three in a
>   Trinity:
> For there is no god except One God (Sura 5:73).

One of the earliest of all the chapters of the Qur'an simply says of God:

> He is Allah, the One and Only;
> Allah the Eternal, Absolute.
> He begetteth not, nor is He begotten (Sura 112:1-3).

However, the Nicene Creed says that Jesus is

> the only-begotten Son of God, begotten of His Father
> before all worlds, God of God, Light of Light, Very God
> of Very God, begotten, not made, being of one substance
> with the Father, by whom all things were made.

So Islam rejects the Trinity, and makes it clear that Allah is not the God and Father of our Lord Jesus Christ. Allah is not Yahweh, not the God defined in the Christian creeds, not the God who is described in the Bible as Father, Son and Holy Spirit, One God.

A special problem: the Trinity

A professor of theology, J.S. Whale, used to deliver a series of lectures to his students in one of the Scottish universities on the doctrine of the Trinity. At the end of the last lecture he would ask: 'Now, have you got it?' and always there was at least one of his students who would reply, confidently, 'Yes!' 'Then', responded Whale, 'you've got it wrong!'

The first thing to be said here is that Christians believe in one God, not three. To the Muslim the doctrine of the Trinity does seem to lead inevitably to three gods. But Christians can stand with the Jews and repeat the 'Shema', 'Hear!': 'Hear O Israel, the Lord our God is ONE', and can stand with the Muslim and repeat the first half of their basic confession of faith, 'There is no god but God.' (Though to be strictly correct that

Christian would *not* be able to say 'There is no god but Allah.) Christians believe in one God.

The formal doctrine of the Trinity, the Three, was not officially adopted by the Church until the Council of Nicea, some three hundred years after the death and resurrection of Jesus. The formula emerged gradually as the Church struggled first with the question of just who Jesus was, and then with the even more difficult question of who the Holy Spirit was. We have to remember that the first Christians were all Jews, all brought up in the tradition of one God. Quickly, faith in Jesus as Lord and Saviour spread to those who were not Jews, and together they had to wrestle with the very difficult question of how they could express their belief in One God and yet affirm Jesus as Lord.

Jesus was clearly more than a man, more than a great teacher, more than a prophet, born of a virgin, risen from the dead and, instead of dying again, ascended into heaven, and then seen, alive, recognisable, by a whole string of witnesses, including five hundred of the Christians at one time (1 Cor. 15:6). They remembered that the accusation brought against him by the Jews was blasphemy, because he 'made himself God.' They called him Lord, which was a title given particularly to Caesar the *divine* ruler but also the title given to God.

But what about the Holy Spirit, the One who completes the Holy Trinity? We find the Three together at the beginning of Matthew's gospel: the Father speaking from heaven, the Son being baptised by John and the Spirit descending 'like a dove' (Mt. 3:13-17). At the end of Matthew's gospel we have the Three again, and again in the context of baptism; the apostles are commanded to make disciples, and to baptise them 'in the name of the Father and of the Son and of the Holy Spirit' (Mt. 28:19). In John's Gospel, Jesus promised the apostles that he would send them 'another Comforter', the Spirit of Truth, the One who would make it possible for them to make disciples because he would 'convict the world of guilt in regard to sin and righteousness and judgment' (Jn. 16:8). Paul brings the Three together in his letter to the Christians at Ephesus: 'There is one body [the Church] and one Spirit [the Holy Spirit] – just as you were called to one hope when you were called – one Lord [Jesus], one faith, one baptism; one God and Father of all' (Eph. 4:4-6).

Christian writers have done their best to produce some satisfactory illustration of how God can be One and yet also Three. An egg has the shell, the white, the yolk, but it's just one egg. Water can be liquid to drink, frozen as ice, and steam to drive an engine, but it's all just water, H_2O. The Trinity has been described as a kind of Divine family, Father and Son, with the Holy Spirit as the love that binds the Three together. Tea may provide a better illustration: it can be a mixture of three different teas but each variety is definitely tea, and the mixture equally is definitely tea. But no illustration really leaves us saying confidently 'Got it!' Or if we do, then we haven't got it!

However, what we must say is that we ought not to be surprised to find that God is rather more complicated than the simple 'One' that we expect. After all, our universe (and he made it) is far more complicated than we had expected, with not just electrons and positrons, but quarks of all sorts and more peculiarities that are being discovered almost daily. If his universe is complex and if the very finest scientists have to admit that they don't have a model to offer us that would enable us to picture it, still less to understand it, then the complexity of God should come as no surprise.

Undoubtedly the Trinity is a big problem for Muslims. Mohamed Al-Nowaihi expresses the problem very clearly:

> It is true that many Muslims have mistakenly believed that Christians worship three separate Gods, and have not paid sufficient attention to the latter's protestation that their belief in the Trinity does not imply a multiplicity of Gods, that God is still one with them. But even when Muslims realise that in the Christian belief the Trinity does not conflict with God's unity, still the most tolerant and broadminded of them fear that it does in some way detract from that absolute oneness and uniqueness.[9]

At the end of this section, I feel that I must remind my reader of the wise words of Gregory of Nazianzus, when he was struggling with trying to understand this problem of the Three in One: 'No sooner do I conceive of the One than I am illumined by the splendour of the Three; no sooner do I distinguish them than I am carried back to the One.'

---

[9] 'The Religion of Islam' in *International Review of Mission* LXV, 258, April 1976, pp216-225.

Chapter four

Rejecting God

The huge problem of human suffering
God and my family
The huge growth of atheism

The huge problem of human suffering

Sadly, many of us close our eyes and our hearts to the world of human suffering. With our eyes closed it is not difficult to believe that the world is a wonderful place, that all things are 'bright and beautiful' and that the Lord God made it all and loves it all. A visit to the Third World (the so-called 'Developing World' which is, in fact, being increasingly crushed in the world's economic mangle) would quickly make us re-assess the situation, as does an accident, an illness, a bereavement.

Of course the world does have its beautiful side. I was on holiday in Scotland and got up very early one morning and went for a quiet walk beside a gently flowing river. And there in front of me, lying peacefully under a tree, was a magnificent stag, its head held high, its polished antlers gleaming, the early morning sun shining through the leaves of the tree and gently dappling its hide. I stood transfixed: 'God, you made that!' I breathed. We've all had those experiences. But I've watched friends die too young, I've conducted the funeral services of babes, I've knelt by the beds of the dying, I went to Northern Ethiopia to help in a famine relief camp. The nurse I was assisting as her interpreter couldn't bring herself to stop work and take a break for a meal and a rest, because she knew that when she stopped the next person waiting to be attended to would surely die. The world has its harsh side, too.

It has been rightly said that no attempt to discuss this problem (the problem of a harsh world and a God who is said to be omnipotent) that does not take into account the awful suffering at Auschwitz can be taken seriously. The apparently limitless potential for human evil is perhaps best illustrated from the records of the Nuremberg War Crimes Tribunal which relate to Auschwitz. In a harrowing account of events at Auschwitz, recorded by I. Greenberg[10], a Polish guard, S. Szmaglewska, was being questioned. He asserted:

> Women carrying children were [always] sent with them to the crematorium. [Children were of no labor value so they were killed. The mothers were sent along, too, because separation might lead to panic, hysteria – which might slow up the destruction process, and this could not be afforded. It was simpler to condemn the mothers too, and keep things quiet and smooth.] The children were then torn from their parents outside the crematorium and sent to the gas chambers separately. [At that

---

[10] In 'Clouds of Smoke, Pillars of Fire,' in E. Fleischner (ed.), *Auschwitz: Beginning of a New Era?* (New York: Klav, 1977), pp9-10.

point, crowding more people into the gas chambers became the most urgent consideration. Separating meant that more children could be packed in separately, or they could be thrown in over the heads of adults once the chamber was packed.] When the extermination of the Jews in the gas chambers was at its height, orders were issued that children were to be thrown straight into the crematorium furnaces, or into a pit near the crematorium, without being gassed first.

The Russian prosecutor asked for clarification: were the children thrown into the furnaces alive or were they first killed?

They threw them in alive. Their screams could be heard at the camp. It is difficult to say how many children were destroyed in this way.

The prosecutor then asked the obvious question: Why?

It's very difficult to say. We don't know whether they wanted to economize on gas, or if it was because there was not enough room in the gas chambers.

Inevitably attempts have been made by Christians to explain why God allowed it to happen. One explanation is the idea of a greater good: that evil brings about some form of good that is much greater than the original evil. It is difficult to see what greater good came from the sufferings of the children thrown alive into the flames. It has been suggested that suffering is character building: that only through our suffering do we grow up, mature. It is certainly arguable that a surfeit of pleasures is likely to turn people away from God simply because they have everything they want, but what character building was there at Auschwitz amongst the women doomed to the gas chambers, bereft of their children?

The free will argument is probably the only satisfactory response to Auschwitz: that in creating us and in giving us freedom to choose, God gave us freedom to choose evil but, in the Christian understanding of things, with the understanding that we will all have to answer, one day, for the choices we have made.

But there is another side to this question of suffering: suffering where it is impossible to blame people for what is happening. On the day after Christmas in 2004 there was an earthquake deep below the Indian Ocean that produced a tidal wave that swept maybe a quarter of a million people into eternity: men, women, little children. An earthquake can't be brought to judgment. So why did God allow it?

Here the answer goes back not to our free will, but to the bondage of the entire universe to law. When the universe was created, and however it was created, it was created subject to laws: the law of gravity, the laws of electricity (Ohm's Law wasn't his: he only discovered God's law governing a particular relationship), the laws governing the reactions between quarks. It is this law-abiding nature of the universe that makes it possible for us to inhabit it (remember, it is an *anthropic* universe, a universe so ordered that at some point we would appear in it). It is those laws which give us the seasons in order: spring, summer, autumn, winter. It is those laws which make ice lighter than water, so that the fish in our ponds can survive freezing temperatures. Without those laws life would be utterly unpredictable: we could not light the gas or turn on the lights without fearing some catastrophe. But those laws also produce earthquakes. God can no more turn off the laws governing nature than he can turn off the free will that governs our nature.

God and my family

The same two answers have to be given to the sufferings that we have all experienced within our families: God cannot take away our free will, so that I am free to abuse my children, and my kitchen stove is bound to burn them if a little finger is poked into a flame. Of course my freedom also allows me to decide whether or not to take the precautions that are sensible around my kitchen: turning the handles of saucepans which contain boiling water in towards the cooker and not outwards where poking little fingers could reach them. And the regularity of the universe allows scientists to develop a switch that will automatically switch off my lawn mower if I run it over the electric cable. But I'm free not to use one of those devices.

Vera (not her actual name) came to me in great distress: her daughter was dying of lung cancer: 'Why does God allow it?' Vera was a Christian: surely God should take care of Christians. But Vera's daughter was a heavy smoker. She knew the danger of it but she exercised her free will to choose to smoke. And God can't deliver us from the consequences of our free choices. *Christianity is not an all-risks covered insurance policy.*

The Traditional Religions would see accidents and illnesses in a different way: they are an indication of the gods' anger because we have omitted some duty owed to them. In other words, the universe is not law-governed, but behind every event, every lightning strike, every rainstorm, every illness, are the gods, warning us, telling us that this is a punishment for an unfulfilled duty. And then one must resort to the wise man, the *shaman*, the 'witch doctor', who will be able to tell me what I have done wrong and what I must do to appease the gods.

Strangely and sadly some Christians fall into this same trap, assuming that good Christians, Bible-believing Christians, should always be happy, always be healthy, even that they should always be wealthy. Then if some tragedy strikes them they assume that it is God punishing them for something they have done wrong. But God simply does not act like that: we all share from time to time in illness and bereavement, and that makes it possible for us to say to others, when they are bereaved or ill, 'I do understand.' But more than that: when things are hard for Christians they do have God to turn to, 'the God of all comfort' (2 Cor. 1:3), and we can point others to that same God who longs to comfort them.

The huge growth of atheism

Although the world presents a bewildering kaleidoscope of religions, arguably the most rapidly growing philosophy of life in the developed world is irreligion, the assertion that there is no God to appeal to, no purpose to look for, no answer to meaninglessness to be found. According to Barrett and Johnson[11], in 1900 there were 226,000 atheists worldwide, but by 2004 this number had leaped to almost 107,000,000. Neither figure can be taken as more than indicative of the situation, but that there has been an enormous growth in unbelief is undeniable.

This development is not to be traced exclusively to the process of education. In the very first century, there were

---

[11] David Barrett and T.M. Johnson, 'Annual Statistical Table on Global Mission 2004', *International Bulletin of Missionary Research*, 28, 1, January 2004.

thinkers enough who poured ridicule on the central beliefs of Christians: the descent of God, a God without the power to deliver himself from the cross, a bodily resurrection and so on. Nor is it to be traced exclusively to the posturing of an anachronistic church, although certainly there is a great gulf separating the church of today with all its pomp and ceremony, from the humble simplicity of the origins of Christianity.[12]

But there is a certain despair amongst thinking people, a belief that nothing can be done to end that strand in all human history that has brought torture, suffering, misery, hunger and death to the masses. Religion appears only to have contributed to human suffering through its religious wars and its prodigious waste of its own material resources. Mother Teresa is an admitted exception, although she, too, had her doubts as to whether God was there at all. A new religion has emerged, or perhaps an old religion has re-emerged, hedonism, characterised by the clubbing culture of young men and women, who set out on Friday nights with the intention of drinking themselves senseless, and with making a hit with some more-or-less willing partner along the way.

In other words for most of these young people this new religion, hedonism, has led them to abandon any search for meaning in life: life does not make sense, life is not fair, if there was a god out there he would put an end to the suffering, but he doesn't, so there isn't. Or

---

[12] There has been a steady flow of books examining the decline of the church in the west. See, for example, Robin Gill, *Beyond Decline* (London: SCM, 1988); Edmund Clowney, *The Church* (Downers Grove: IVP, 1995); Tobin Gamble, *The Irrelevant Church* (Monarch, 1991); Donald Reeves (ed.), *The Church and the State* (London: Hodder & Stoughton, 1984).

perhaps the argument is different: science has made religion unnecessary and untenable. Or perhaps there is no conscious attempt to discover any meaning to life, and life is lived out in a blind following of what others are doing. Togetherness is important, peer pressure is powerful, and it's best to give in to it.

Perhaps it should be said that a good part of the blame for this growth of atheism must be placed fairly and squarely on the Church. We spend too much time in discussing our questions, and too little time trying to answer the real questions that are being asked out there, amongst the clubbers and binge drinkers. Worse still we either give the wrong answers or we simply join the crowd and admit that we don't have any answer: 'God's ways are not our ways.' The situation can in good measure be traced back to the theological colleges, where pressure on the curriculum means that the study of ethics, including crucial issues such as suffering, often get squeezed out by the demands of other studies. The courses on offer need to help students face up to the real issues and find credible answers.

Chapter five

One God in many religions?

The three monos: Judaism, Islam and Christianity
Hinduism and Buddhism
The Traditional Religions
Allah, Yahweh, Krishna, Buddha, Waq
All right? All wrong? Only one right?
Six explanations of religions

The three monos: Judaism, Islam and Christianity

Judaism

Judaism is the faith associated with the first covenant. Its history is written in the Jewish Bible, the Christian Old Testament. If it has its origins in any one person that person is Abraham, although Moses is arguably of much more significance to the Jewish people because of his involvement in the Exodus from Egypt and his part in receiving the Jewish Law at Sinai.

Judaism is strictly and unequivocally monotheistic. Its core belief is summed up in the *Shema*: 'Hear, O Israel, the Lord our God is One Lord.' He reveals his name to them, 'Yahweh' (Ex. 3:13-14), a word which is usually translated as 'I am who I am.' The name is a little bleak: it seems to carry a warning: don't ask too many questions about me: I am what I am. As we have seen, the Jews seemed to sense that warning and so never pronounced the Name. This may well explain the fact that when Jesus said 'before Abraham was born, *I am*' it was taken to be blasphemous (Jn. 8:58-59).

Through their history the Jewish people were confident that they were a very special people, chosen by God. But they were also painfully aware that their history seemed to be a long history of slavery, of persecution, their land repeatedly occupied by other nations. But there was hope: Yahweh would send another deliverer, another Moses, a Messiah, one who was anointed like the priests and the kings but anointed, set apart to be Israel's 'redeemer.'

There is a danger when we read the New Testament that we will find more than is really there. The Jews expected a Messiah but they certainly did not expect God himself; they expected someone to come to get rid of their Roman oppressors but they did not expect someone to come to get rid of their sins. And that was a problem for Paul and the other apostles when they came to preach in the Jewish synagogues: they could proclaim that Jesus was the Messiah and they could point to his resurrection as proof, but then they had to show from the Jewish Bible, the Old Testament, that the Messiah was to be a suffering Messiah, not a battling Messiah; a Man of peace and not a man of war. So, in Antioch Paul insisted that 'in condemning him (Jesus) they fulfilled the words of the prophets that are read every Sabbath' . . . but 'God raised him from the dead, and for many days he was seen by those who had travelled with him' (Acts 13:27,30,31). Paul went on to show from the Jewish Bible that the resurrection was not some new idea but was actually prophesied in Psalm 16. At Thessalonica Paul went to the synagogue and 'on three Sabbath days he reasoned with them from the Scriptures, explaining and proving that the Christ (the Greek word for the Anointed One) had to suffer and rise from the dead' (Acts 17:2-3).

It is perhaps surprising that although the Jewish people expected a human messiah-deliverer, it never occurred to them to think that God himself might appear to them as he had done in the past. After their escape from Egypt the Israelites paused at Sinai to receive their Law. And then 'Moses and Aaron, Nadab and Abihu, and the seventy elders of Israel went up and saw the God of Israel' (Ex. 24:9). In Genesis 16 we find Hagar running away from Abram and Sarai because of Sarai's treatment of her. Then 'the angel of the Lord' found her and promised that her son Ishmael would receive God's blessing, a blessing similar to the one promised to Abram himself. And Hagar 'gave this name to the Lord who spoke to her: "You are the God who sees me," for she said, "I have now seen the One who sees me"' (Gen. 16:13).

In the Old Testament is there any indication of a God who is One and yet Three? It is sometimes suggested that Genesis 1:26, 'Let us make man in our image, in our likeness' is just such an indication, but this is probably no more than the 'us' and 'we' that royalty have used for centuries: in fact until very recently Kings and Queens of England never used 'I' when they made public speeches but always said 'we'. However there is reference even earlier in that chapter of Genesis to 'the Spirit of God' who was 'hovering over the waters' (Gen. 1:2), and this same 'Spirit of God' appears again in the account of the building of the Tent of Meeting, the Tabernacle. God says 'I have chosen Bezalel son of Huri . . . and I have filled him with the Spirit of God' (Ex. 31:2-3), words which at once seem to link up with the experience of the apostles at Pentecost, when they were 'all filled with the Spirit.' So we might well be tempted to put together the Angel of the Lord and the Spirit of God and Yahweh who sent that Spirit and see there an indication at least of the Trinity. But it is the fact that the Jews never took that step, and never modified their cardinal belief: 'the Lord our God is One Lord.'

In Old Testament times the Jewish people depended on sacrifice to deal with their sins. In the New Testament, however, the letter to the Hebrews says flatly that 'it is impossible for the blood of bulls and goats to take away sins.' From the Christian standpoint, the Jewish people were formed as a cradle for the coming of Jesus, and as the forerunner of the worldwide church. There was a famous experiment by Pavlov in which he demonstrated what he called a conditioned reflex. Before he fed his dogs he rang a bell. Soon the dogs associated the ringing of the bell with their meal, and their mouths watered in preparation. But when that reflex was well established their mouths watered whenever they heard a bell, whether it was before they were to be fed or not. It was a conditioned, an automatic, reflex action. Through the sacrifices a kind of conditioned reflex was being produced in the Jewish people; whenever they encountered sin they at once thought of sacrifice. So when the death of Jesus was proclaimed to them they didn't find the idea of sacrifice for sin difficult at all.

What they did find difficult was the idea that their Messiah should be a sacrifice. They thought he would be a political deliverer to get rid of the Romans. And here we find a second aspect of the Jewish people: they were given the Scriptures, and especially they were given the prophets. So when Paul and the other apostles began announcing that Jesus was a crucified sacrifice for sin they could immediately find prophecies that proved the point. Isaiah chapter 53 became a favourite text for that purpose:

> He was despised and rejected by men,
> a man of sorrows, and familiar with suffering.
> Like one from whom men hide their faces
> he was despised, and we esteemed him not.
> Surely he took up our infirmities and carried our sorrows,
> yet we considered him stricken by God,
> smitten by him, and afflicted.
> But he was pierced for our transgressions,
> he was crushed for our iniquities;
> the punishment that brought us peace was upon him,
> and by his wounds we are healed (Is. 53:3-5).

It is not surprising that all of the apostles and most of the first Christians were Jews. Bishop Stephen Neill once asked the Jews a very important question:

> Is Judaism something which exists for the Jews alone? Or is it something which they hold in trust for the whole of mankind? If the latter, how do they understand their universal mission, and in what terms would they wish to exercise it in relation to the rest of the world?[13]

---

[13] Stephen Neill, *Christian Faith and Other Faiths* (Oxford: OUP, 1961), p29.

I was interested in this question myself. Some years ago I was involved in a television programme which included a conversation between me and the Principal of a London based Jewish college. While we were waiting for the filming to begin we walked in the grounds of the college, and I asked: 'Do you believe in heaven?' He replied yes, he did. Then I asked, 'But how am I to get there?' He replied 'Through your own religion.' I knew that this was not the orthodox answer, so I challenged him: 'That's not what you really believe, is it?' 'No!' 'So, how do I get to heaven, how do I get into the Kingdom?' 'By obeying the Covenant of Noah.'

Actually I already knew that from my reading, but had wondered how widespread that idea was. The Covenant of Noah was the covenant Yahweh gave to Noah after the flood, in Genesis 9:1-17. In fact the seven Noachide Laws are derived from Yahweh's promises to Adam and to Noah. Jews are required to observe the whole Torah, the Law, but non-Jews must accept the seven laws of the Noah Covenant as coming from God. Firstly, positively, mankind must establish a legal system. The other six laws are prohibitions: no idolatry, blasphemy, bloodshed, sexual sins, theft and (oddly) no eating meat from a living animal. This last prohibition just might refer to Ethiopia, where various travellers in the past reported that at some feasts flesh was cut from living animals, and eaten raw. Just possibly Ethiopians might have travelled to Jerusalem and carried on the practice there, or the Jewish people might have heard (to their horror: eating flesh with blood was forbidden to them) of the practice in Ethiopia.

Salvation becomes a matter of obeying laws, something which we find we cannot, in fact, do.

Islam

Muhammad recognised the absurdity of the religion of
the Arabs of his day. In Mecca was the Ka'ba, a storehouse for the three hundred and more idols worshipped
by the various tribes. His grandfather was appointed
Guardian of the Ka'ba, a very important position to
hold. Muhammad would have none of it. Having travelled to Syria and seen the monotheism of the Jews he
came to Mecca asserting: 'There is no god but Allah.'
Actually he did not invent that name for God: his father
was named Abdullah, abd-allah, 'Servant of Allah', and
the Arabs seem to have believed that behind all the idols
there was this One whom they called Al-ilah, 'The God'.
But as in nearly all the Traditional Religions this One,
'The God', was far too important to be involved in the
ordinary affairs of life, and could safely be ignored. It
was the gods who really mattered, not God. Muhammad
put Allah in the centre and banished the rest.

   Just once Muhammad was tempted to compromise
over this 'one' principle. His early converts were being
persecuted, and to ease their sufferings he seems to have
decided to give some place to the three most important
female sky-deities of the Meccans, Al-Lat, Al-Uzza and
Manat: they could be trusted as intercessors. This seems
to have satisfied a good many Meccans, who adopted
this modified form of Muhammad's religion. But
Muhammad soon realised that he had taken away the
very foundation stone of Islam, and took back his words.
Sura 53 of the Qur'an states:

> Have ye seen Lat and Uzza and another, the Third (god-
>   dess), Manat?
> What! For you the male sex, and for Him the female?
> Behold, such would be indeed a division most unfair!

These are nothing but names which ye have devised –
For which Allah has sent down no authority (whatever)
(Sura 53:19-23).

The incident was made the centre piece of Salman
Rushdie's book *The Satanic Verses*.[14] The title of the book
comes from a common Muslim explanation of what happened, that Muhammad never did offer a role for the
three goddesses, but Satan interjected the words while
Muhammad was speaking, and so his listeners thought
that Muhammad had said them. The whole story is
recorded in Alfred Guillaume's translation of the earliest
biography of Muhammad that we have.[15]

Islam is built on a quadrilateral; there are four authorities
which together provide the Muslim with the *sunna*, the
pathway first trod by Muhammad and now to be trodden
by all Muslims. The most important is the Qur'an.
However, there are contradictions within the Qur'an, and
so we have to add the second authority: abrogation. This is
the principle that says that Allah can abrogate, cancel out a
verse of the Qur'an already given, and replace it with something else. The earlier verse is cancelled by a later verse.
Unfortunately it is extremely difficult to decide the dates
when particular verses were given. But this idea of abrogation explains how it is that Muslims can show from the
Qur'an both that it teaches peace and that it teaches war. It
all depends on how the verses are dated: do the peace verses cancel out the war verses or is it the other way round?

The third authority is Tradition (*hadith*). These traditions are the record of what people remembered

---

[14] Salman Rushdie, *The Satanic Verses* (London: Viking, 1988).
[15] Alfred Guillaume, *The Life of Muhammad* (Oxford: OUP,
1955), pp165-167. Ibn Ishaq died in 773AD, rather more
than one hundred years after the death of Muhammad.

Muhammad saying and doing. There are hundreds of them, with the collection by Bukhari being probably the most important collection. Fourthly there is the Shari'a Law: not, in fact, one law but several systems of law, all based on the first three authorities. Fundamental to Islam is the One God, Allah.

For the Muslim, Allah can best be known through his names, ninety-nine of them. He is Al-Malik, 'King', Al-Rahman, 'The Most Gracious', Al-Fatir, 'Creator', Al-Qayyum, 'The Eternal', Al-Alim, 'The All-Knowing'. Muslims recite the ninety-nine names using a rosary, a string of one hundred beads. It is popularly said that only the camel knows the hundredth name of Allah, and that explains the camel's supercilious look.

Importantly for the Muslim, Allah is Al-Ghaffar, 'The Forgiver'. Since there is no redeemer in Islam, and no sacrificial system to deal with sin, the Muslim depends for his salvation on obedience to the way set out by Muhammad, the Sunna. But Muslims know that they never manage completely to conform to that Sunna, so they fall back on good works, such as feeding beggars, to set against their shortcomings, and on the intercession of Muslim saints, but ultimately on Al-Ghaffar, 'The Forgiver'. The hope is that since Allah is the Forgiver he will simply forgive the sinner, perhaps in recognition of the fact that the sinner has done his best to follow the life-style of Muhammad, to live according to Sunna.

There is obviously a contrast here between God in Christianity, whose justice cannot merely pass over, forget, sin. Justice requires that every sin should carry with it a particular consequence (Heb. 2:1-3). By ourselves we can't hope to escape from those consequences. Indeed, Paul boldly comments that God's justice was challenged by the fact that over the centuries before the coming of Jesus he did not deal with sin (Rom. 3:25-26). However, the challenge has been met by the coming of Jesus at God's appointed time, to die for those past unpunished sins and for the sins of the whole world.

Muhammad used the word *jahiliyya* to describe the state of the Arab people before Islam: 'ignorance'. His early message to them was simple: there is only one God, care for the poor, the widow, the orphan (he was one). Don't exploit anyone. But gradually this simple message was expanded and a complex system emerged, with the focus on the five pillars: prayer to be performed five times each day, the affirmation 'There is no god but Allah and Muhammad is his messenger', fasting in the month of Ramadan (when Muhammad had first claimed to have received Allah's revelations), pilgrimage to Mecca (oddly enough with the focus on the Ka'ba, the old storehouse for idols), and giving alms to the mosque, for the poor.

Controversially the Qur'an affirms the virgin birth of Jesus, but denies that he was crucified. In Sura 4 of the Qur'an the Jews are accused because:

> They rejected faith, that they uttered against Mary a grave false charge,
> that they said (in boast) 'We killed Christ Jesus the son of Mary, the messenger of Allah' –
> but they killed him not, nor crucified him (Sura 4:156-7).

This denial of the crucifixion is not a question of theology, but a question of history: either Jesus was crucified, and the Bible is right, or Jesus was *not* crucified, and the Qur'an is right. A Muslim scholar, Seyyed Hossein Nasr, has put it very clearly:

> The Qur'an does not accept that Jesus was crucified, but states that he was taken directly to heaven. This is the

one irreducible 'fact' separating Christianity from Islam, a fact which is in reality placed there providentially to prevent a mingling of the two religions.[16]

One of the more striking ways of seeing the difference between Islam and Christianity is to compare Jesus and Muhammad.

- Jesus was born by the virgin Mary, Muhammad was born some five hundred years later, the son of Abdullah and Amina.
- Jesus grew up in rural Nazareth: Muhammad grew up in urban Mecca.
- Jesus lived under Roman occupation: Muhammad lived in independent Arabia.
- Jesus came from a poor family of little significance: Muhammad's grandfather was Guardian of the Ka'ba, his uncle was head of the Hashimite clan.
- Jesus never married: Muhammad had at least twelve wives.
- Jesus is recorded as having performed many miracles: Muhammad claimed only what he called the miracle of the Qur'an (although later pious Muslims credited him with miracles).
- Jesus was a man of peace: Muhammad was personally engaged in at least 26 battles and was wounded in one of them.
- Jesus was crucified at the age of thirty-two or thereabouts: Muhammad died of natural causes, in the arms of his favourite wife Aisha, at the age of sixty-three.
- Jesus rose from death and ascended to heaven: Muhammad's tomb is in Medina.

---

[16] Seyyed Hossein Nasr, *Islamic Life and Thought* (London: Allen and Unwin, 1981), p209.

• In his lifetime Jesus appeared to be a failure: Muhammad was an undoubted success.

Clearly there is a great contrast between Islam and Christianity and this contrast is brought into focus by the contrast between Muhammad and Jesus: Muhammad the prophet, with a normal birth and death, Jesus the incarnate Son of God, coming into the world through a virgin birth, leaving this world by way of the cross, triumphing over death, designated Son of God with power by the resurrection (Rom. 1:1-4), ascended and glorified, some day to return in glory.

In the twenty-first century we find a worldwide re-awakening of Islam. We can date this from Gamal Abdul Nasser and his resistance in 1957 to France, Britain and Israel when they attempted to take over the Suez Canal. He became a hero to the Muslim world, which realised that Islam could resist the West. Muslims had been puzzled by their experience: after centuries of political success, and Muslim empire after Muslim empire they were, in the twentieth century, apparently powerless.

This is perhaps nowhere better illustrated than Winston Churchill's own description of how he and a few others carved up the Middle East:

> In the spring of 1923 I was sent to the Colonial Office, to take over our business in the Middle East, and bring matters into some kind of order . . . I therefore convened a conference at Cairo to which practically all the experts and authorities of the Middle East were summoned. Accompanied by Lawrence [of Arabia], Hubert Young and Trenchard from the Air Ministry, I set out for Cairo . . . We submitted the following main proposals to the Cabinet. First we would repair the injury done to the Arabs and to the House of the Sherifs of Mecca by placing

the Emir Feisal upon the throne of Iraq as King, and by entrusting the Emir Abdullah with the government of Transjordania. Secondly we would remove practically all the troops from Iraq and entrust its defence to the Royal Air Force. Thirdly, we suggested an adjustment of the immediate difficulties between the Jews and Arabs in Palestine which would serve as a foundation for the future.[17]

Churchill's plans were implemented, and inevitably provoked opposition, rioting, violence. In 1931 Colonel (later Field Marshal) Montgomery, as Commander in Chief of all British forces in Palestine, was desperately trying to keep the lid on the pot of unrest that threatened at any moment to boil over.[18] Some eighty years on these events have an amazing resonance with the preoccupations of today's politicians. They indicate the gulf separating the Middle East of Churchill's day, when Arab peoples could be governed and dominated without particular reference to them, and the Middle East today, with its assertive and combative Arab rulers.

1957 saw the turn of the tide. Islam awakened, and some, at least, of the Muslims thought once again of their vision of Islam as a success, not a failure, as leading the whole world into submission to Allah. Bishop Stephen Neill explains the difference on this point between Christian and Muslim ways of thinking:

> Let us put it quite crudely. Jesus was a failure and Muhammad was a success. The Gospel was from the

---

[17] Winston Churchill, *Great Contemporaries* (London: Fontana, 1937), pp131-132.
[18] See Nigel Hamilton, *Monty* (London: Hodder & Stoughton, 1981), chapter 6.

start a story of victory arising out of defeat. For centuries the Christians were a minority of insignificant and persecuted people; they saw the miracle of progress as a direct act of God, who uses the weak things of the world to confound the strong . . . The Church will be to the end of time a persecuted Church; the purpose of God will be fulfilled slowly and obscurely . . .

Very different is the outlook of the Muslim. He has been brought up on a success story. Muhammad was a great leader of men. Finding the Arab tribes of the eighth century weak, divided and purposeless, through the force of his personality and his creed he knit them into a unity, gave them a social organization and launched them on an astonishing career of conquest. Within a century of the death of the Prophet the Muslims had taken over Persia, Mesopotamia, Syria, Egypt, North Africa and the greater part of Spain . . . [19]

Here is a major difference between Christianity and Islam: the role of violence. Jesus warned his followers, that 'all who draw the sword will die by the sword' (Mt. 26:52), but Muhammad might fairly be termed a violent man, engaged personally in 26 or 27 battles. The trajectory of violence in the early history of Islam is described by Reuven Firestone:

At the beginning of his prophetic career in Mecca when (Muhammad) was weak and his followers few, the divine revelations encouraged avoidance of physical conflict. Only after the intense physical persecution that resulted in the Emigration (Hijra) of the Muslim

---

[19] Stephen Neill, *Christian Faith and Other Faiths* (London: OUP, 1961), pp41-42.

community to Medina in 622 were Muhammad and the
believers given divine authority to engage in war and
only in defence. As the Muslim community continued
to grow in numbers and strength in Medina, further
revelations widened the conditions and narrowed the
restrictions under which war could be waged, until it
was concluded that war against non-Muslims could be
waged virtually at any time, without pretext and in any
place.[20]

The heady reality of military success in the past and the
experience of two centuries of weakness and failure in
good measure lie behind the rise of Islamists, the
jihadists, those who emphasise jihad, in the sense that
Muhammad used the word as physical conflict. Sayyid
Qutb, the Egyptian Islamist, executed by the Egyptian
government in 1966 because of his subversive activities,
is today, the most influential writer of the time for the
Muslim radicals. He explained *jihad*, 'struggle', as follows:

> The Muslim community was raised to assume the lead-
> ership of humanity . . . the Muslim community must
> undertake to oppose any power that would stand in its
> way and prevent it from conveying the message freely to
> the public, or would threaten its followers. The Muslim
> community must pursue this course of jihad or struggle
> for God's cause, until all threat of oppression is elimi-
> nated and people are free to believe in and practice
> Islam.
> This is the true jihad, as recognised and endorsed by
> Islam. Those who take part in it are richly rewarded and

---

[20] Reuven Firestone, *Jihad* (New York and Oxford: Oxford
University Press, 1999), p50.

rank among the noblest of believers, and those who give their lives in doing so are the true martyrs.[21]

Qutb's explanation of the two centuries of the near eclipse of Muslim power was simple: they had abandoned Islam as Muhammad had presented it in favour of a pale copy of western materialism. Just as before the birth of Muhammad the Arab world was living through an era of ignorance (he used the term *jahiliyya*), so over the centuries Islam, all of it, has returned to jahiliyya. The inevitable consequence was the failure of all the promises of the Qur'an, all the expectations that Islam would overcome the whole world. The answer was a return to their roots, and a return to jihad. Here Qutb appealed to the example of Muhammad, who would not tolerate apostasy, who spread the influence of Islam, who lived much of his life by the power of the sword. It seems that Qutb would have approved of the suicide bombers, the new 'martyrs' of the Islamic jihad.

The Roman Catholic Church may be allowed to sum up the views of Christianity with regard to Islam. Positively, Vatican Council II identified five authentic elements of Muslim spirituality:

> They worship God who is one, living and subsistent, merciful and almighty, the Creator of heaven and earth, who has also spoken to men. They strive to submit themselves without reserve to the hidden decrees of God . . . Although not acknowledging Him as God, they revere Jesus as a prophet . . . they await the day of judgement and the reward of God following the resurrection of the dead. For this reason they highly esteem the upright life,

---

[21] Sayyid Qutb, *In the Shade of the Qur'an* vol. 1 (Leicester: The Islamic Foundation, 1999), pp208-9.

and worship God, especially by way of prayer, alms-deeds and fasting.[22]

But it is what was not said by the Vatican II document that is more significant. Thirty years after Vatican II, Pope John-Paul II commented:

> The religiosity of Muslims deserves respect. It is impossible not to admire, for example, their fidelity to prayer. Some of the most beautiful names in the human language are given to God in the Koran, but He is ultimately a God outside of the world, a God who is only Majesty, never Emmanuel, God with us . . . There is no room for the Cross and the resurrection. Jesus is mentioned, but only as a prophet . . . not only the theology but also the anthropology of Islam is very distant from Christianity.[23]

Christianity

Although it has its roots in the Old Testament and therefore in Judaism, Christianity has Jesus as its ultimate foundation. When in the early days of Christianity the Church's thinkers had time to absorb and study the life and teaching of Jesus, and the comments of the apostles who had been with him for those three tumultuous years, they were able to come up with a startling explanation of what Christianity was.

Firstly there was the recognition that Jesus was the Messiah (from the Hebrew), the Christ (from the Greek),

---

[22] A. Flannery, *Vatican Council II: The Conciliar and Post Conciliar Documents* (Dublin: Dominican Publications, 1975), *Nostra Aetate*, p740.

[23] Pope John-Paul II, *Crossing the Threshold of Hope* (London: Jonathan Cape, 1994), p93.

the Anointed One, anointed as priest, as prophet, as King, and as sacrifice. Crucially, Jesus was no mere man, although he had truly become man. But in Jesus we had God incarnate, God in human flesh. Born miraculously, at God's chosen time, of a virgin, crucified, dead, buried, risen, ascended, at a time ordained by God and prophesied in the Old Testament Scriptures. His death and resurrection provided humanity not with a new set of laws but with a sacrifice for sins, a sacrifice to be accepted by faith and through the sheer grace of God. And we were not to be left alone to work this out for ourselves. There was a Third, the Paraclete, the Holy Spirit, who would make it possible for us to live the kind of lives we have always wanted to live. In a remarkable re-appraisal of the nature of God, those early Christian thinkers recognised that the One God was both One and Three, Father, Son, Holy Spirit.

All this was Good News, and the task of the Church was to take that Good News to everyone. This was no religion to be kept for one nation, but Good News for all nations. So in the footsteps of Paul, missionaries were to set out to announce the Good News.

But with all this decided, the Church took a wrong turning. With the apparent conversion of the Roman Emperor Constantine in 312, Christianity became first tolerated and then adopted as the religion of the empire. Christians were not merely allowed in the Roman army: *only* Christians were allowed in the army. In fact the Church was almost adopted by the State, given recognition and respect by the State, and Christian leaders began to deal on equal terms with the State. The distinction between politics and the Church became blurred: in fact the Church was politicised. Of course Islam had always been both 'a religious and a political entity.' And so, inevitably, politicised Christianity came into violent

collision with politicised Islam with the Crusades as just
one almost inevitable consequence. Everywhere the border of successive Muslim Caliphates was a border with
either the Western Church, based on Rome, or the
Eastern Church, based on Constantinople. The Church
might be said to have adopted the words supposedly
seen by Constantine, written in the sky: *hoc signo victor
eris*, 'In this sign you will conquer,' but to have forgotten
that the sign was the sign of the cross, not the sign of the
sword.

Christianity had and has always had Jesus as its ultimate foundation. But on this foundation there have been
built an amazing assortment of more-or-less systematic
theologies which have been attached to a parallel assortment of denominations. The first division separated out
the Eastern Church (based on Constantinople) and the
Western Church (based on Rome). The Eastern portion
divided into the Eastern Orthodox churches (including
the Russian and Greek churches) and the Oriental
Orthodox churches (including the Egyptian, Ethiopian
and Syrian churches). The Western portion also split,
with the Church of England repudiating Rome, only to
be itself split when the Methodists and the Baptists, and
the Congregationalists and the Brethren went their separate ways.

In Continental Europe in the sixteenth century there
was the Reformation, with Martin Luther in Germany
and the younger John Calvin in Switzerland, and not a
few lesser luminaries, going back behind the accumu-
lated traditions of the Church and formulating new theologies, spreading new ideas about the nature of
Christianity.

What is interesting here is that despite their differences they are all quite evidently Christian. The Roman
Catholic Church has a Pope, bishops, priests, baptism

and communion, but the Salvation Army (which, despite its protestations that it is not a church, is church to hundreds of thousands) has none of them. It is the very fact that Christianity has no one authoritative structure that has enabled it to cross cultural barriers and establish itself in every corner of the world.

Hinduism and Buddhism

These two mainly Asian religions are difficult to describe: both offer a pick-'n-mix variety of forms. Hinduism is essentially the package of religions originating in India, in the Indus valley. At least in theory the package is bound together by a belief in re-incarnation: death is not the end of life, but a doorway to another life, one that will be better than the present life or worse than the present life depending on one's *karma*, how one has lived in this life and how one lived in previous lives. Karma is a law which governs every action because every action has an eternal consequence. What that consequence is, is determined by *dharma*, 'duty'. Any action that is in accordance with dharma has a positive effect on one's future, and every action contrary to dharma has a negative effect. The person will, in the next incarnation, come back richer or poorer, as a man or a woman, or even as an animal, depending on what we might call the balance of karma carried forward.

The Hindu, in fact, was endowed with an inescapable eternal life. Since life in India was rarely anything more than tolerable, some means of escape from the cycle of existence, the *Samsaric Cycle*, had to be found, and was to be found in withdrawal from the world, self-denial, devotion to the gods and general asceticism, all activities that were beyond the possibilities for ordinary people, who were too occupied with scratching out a living to give much time to philosophy and meditation.

Consequently Hinduism developed along two lines, a more philosophical line, which tried to reduce the gods of the Hindu sacred texts, the Vedas, to some kind of generally monotheistic order, and folk Hinduism which recognised the deities of the Vedas but restricted itself to the service of the respective village gods. On the one hand, but very much in the background, was the notion of gods who created and re-created the worlds, but on the other hand was *this* god whose temper depended on how well he has been served by our villagers.

For the orthodox and philosophically minded Hindu, Brahma is the Absolute, not personal, not the creator of the universe (because the universe is eternal, it was not created.) Brahma is the totality of everything that really is, everything that is not illusion, *maya*. The eternal element of every human being is a part of Brahma. Brahma is associated with two others, Vishnu and Shiva, to make a kind of high Hindu trinity. Vishnu is the Preserver but Shiva is the Destroyer, and Brahma acts as a kind of balancing force between them. Each of these has a female consort. But then one must somehow find a place for the multitude of village gods. Clearly we are a long way from One God.

Buddhism developed out of Hinduism through Siddharta Gautama, generally referred to as the Buddha, 'The Enlightened'. He found Hinduism too philosophical, too complicated. He seems to have been brought up in luxury, cut off from the harsh realities of the life of the poor. Tradition says that this isolation was imposed on him by his father because of a prophecy that he would grow up and as a consequence of certain signs he would see he would retire from the world.

Some five hundred years before the birth of Jesus, tiring of the restricted life of his father's estates, Gautama went out with his servant, and saw the predicted signs: an old man, a dead man, a sick man and a monk. The first three frightened him: he had never been allowed to see such things before. The fourth sign intrigued him: how was this monk so serene, so untroubled? Gautama left his wife and child and went out in search of understanding, an understanding of suffering and of how to escape from it. He tried asceticism, and nearly killed himself with the rigour of his practices, but asceticism took him no further in his search for understanding. He studied philosophy, but that, too, failed to satisfy him.

He claimed to have received enlightenment while sitting in the shade of a fig tree, later called the Bo or Bodhi tree, 'The Tree of Enlightenment'. His theology was simple:

- all existence involves suffering
- suffering is caused by desire
- if we put an end to desire, to wanting things, then the suffering will also end
- the way to end desire is by following a middle way, neither wanting things nor not wanting things. Since it is desire and suffering which tie us to this world, ending desire would ultimately bring *nirvana*, extinction.

But what is extinction? It is like the flame of a candle being blown out: it has been extinguished, but it is pointless to ask where the flame has gone. That submission to ignorance is fine for philosophers, but the rest of us want to know where the 'flame' has gone, what happens to me after my death? Is God out there? Is anything out there?

Gautama himself was an agnostic: he wouldn't say whether there were gods or a God or no gods. For him, as in Hinduism, there is an ultimate reality (and the real 'me' is part of that reality), but whether it is in any sense 'god' is uncertain. The package of beliefs offered by Gautama was not very satisfying to the average Buddhist, and through the centuries after his death Buddhism divided, with traditional beliefs enshrined in Theravada Buddhism (which was contemptuously called Hinayana, 'the lesser vehicle' by more progressive Buddhists) left to the monks and philosophers and Mahayana, 'the greater vehicle', Buddhism being for everyone else. Instead of *nirvana* there was paradise, and instead of an agnostic Gautama we have a Buddha to be worshipped. So in Buddhism we seem to arrive at an agnostic 'god'.

Mahayana Buddhism produced the Pure-Land sect. Here once again we can see how the expectations of the people will mould religion so that it meets their needs. A Buddhist monk named Dharmakara is supposed to have heard about Paradise from an enlightened one, a Buddha. He promised that when he attained enlightenment he would create a new and far better paradise, and that anyone who believed in him and called on his name, would gain that paradise. He is known as the Amida-Buddha; some claim that in an earlier existence he was Buddha-Gautama.

There is an intriguing third stream in Buddhism, Zen Buddhism. This developed amongst the Chinese, who wanted to get back to the original form of Buddhism and the pathway of Gautama the Buddha. They knew that, according to tradition, Gautama was looking for enlightenment and that suddenly it came to him, while he was sitting under that fig tree. The true follower of the Buddha, then, was not someone who followed a set of rules but a person who looked for enlightenment, for that flash of understanding that can suddenly resolve a paradox, point to the solution to a problem.

Zen monasteries have a meditation hall and set times for meditation. Some Zen Buddhists make use of yoga, which is *not*, as some westerners believe, a form of physical exercise but a control mechanism for dismissing first the body and then the mind, so that one is empty and therefore in a condition to be filled with enlightenment. Others make use of the *koan*, a paradoxical statement, often apparent nonsense: 'meditate on the sound of one hand clapping.' The koan may be a riddle: 'a man kept a goose in a bottle. It grew fatter and fatter, until it could no longer get out of the bottle. What did the man do?' The Zen answer to the riddle would precisely *not* be a common sense and practical answer to the riddle ('Break the bottle!'). It would come with a flash of enlightenment and might not make any apparent sense at all.

Once again we are forced to reject the notion that somehow all religions are basically the same: Buddhist ideas and practices are a far cry from those of Islam or Judaism or Christianity or the Traditional Religions.

The Traditional Religions

Until recently almost everyone in the world has been religious. In Africa and Asia and the Americas, people somehow put together explanations of how the world began, how people ought to live, what happens when we die and, inevitably, some explanation of human suffering. These are the Traditional Religions. Obviously they differ from one another in many details but there are three beliefs basic to them all: that life ought to be orderly, that the world is causal and that humanity is the focus of the world.

Life ought to be orderly, and so the task of religion is to restore order when it breaks down. A flood is disorderly but so is disease. A house on fire is disorderly and so is death. In each case, religion must restore order and this is done by relentlessly asking 'Why?' The scientific world asks 'How?' but Traditional Religions go behind that question to ask 'Why?'

Life is causal. Traditional Religions say that life is causal, by which they mean that everything that happens is caused . . . but not merely in the scientific sense. When the scientist points to tectonic plates and the earth's cooling to explain the Tsunami disaster of 2004, the Traditional Religions are interested but not impressed: one can't argue with the laws of nature so as to restore order.

Humanity is the focus of the world. For the Traditional Religions the real questions are all 'Why?' questions, questions people ask, because people are the focus of all that happens. The big question with respect to the Tsunami is 'Why was James in the path of the tidal wave but Jenny was not?' Again, what caused the Tsunami was not ultimately the laws of science but the behaviour of people. They must now be helped to correct that behaviour and so to restore order. Interestingly, Islam gave much the same answer to the Tsunami disaster as did the Traditional Religions: the Tsunami was a punishment from Allah for the pleasure-seeking immoral westerners who holidayed in the area.

This need to correct one's behaviour takes us to the gods of the Traditional Religions. Disorder is a sign of their displeasure. Something has been done to displease them: a sacrifice not offered, a visit to a grave not made, a house built in some novel way or in an unexpected place, food cooked in the wrong pot: any of these might be the cause of disorder. The wise man, the *shaman*, the 'witch doctor', is the one who can discover the source of the disorder and can determine what action needs to be taken.

It is ultimately the Shaman who lays down the morality of the community. There is a right way to do everything: a right way to build a house, to plough a field, to sow the crops, to cook a meal, to bear a child, to bury the dead, and each right way is associated with morality. The right way is right not because it is the most effective way or the most convenient way, but because the history of the people has shown that it is the safe way, the way approved by the gods, the way that does not bring disaster to the people.

Traditional Religions almost invariably seem to have a belief in a High God, a Sky God, a Supreme Creator, but because of his greatness he is not usually to be imagined as being involved in the day-to-day life of the people. In fact most Traditional Religions have some account of a kind of 'Fall', some act of the people that caused God to move away from them. The Ashanti of Ghana say that it was the noise made by the women with their pestles and mortars, grinding grain, that drove God away. Others say that it was the chattering of the women at the river when they went to fetch water, or even the smoke from their fires that caused God to go away. It's interesting that the blame is usually put on the women rather than the men! Whatever reason is given it is usually believed that the creator God is now far distant from us.

But there is usually another figure, a lesser god. In southern Ethiopia sacrifices are offered to Doressa when things go wrong, but little mention is ever made of Magano. Magano is the remote Creator, Doressa is the near-at-hand mischief maker, always ready to take offence and then to punish the offender. Actually when

Christianity came to these people they identified Magano as God, but Doressa as Satan.

This idea of the distant God is interesting, because in Kenya and Uganda and other places where the Traditional Religions were in place, when the Christian missionaries came and talked about Jesus, the people found that the idea of his sacrifice on the cross was easy to accept, but the really good news was that their distant god had come back close to them.

Allah, Yahweh, Krishna, Buddha, Waq

In Islam the name is Allah, 'The God', in Judaism it is the Name that must not be named, Yahweh, in Hinduism we have Krishna and Brahma and Shiva, in Buddhism we have Gautama the Enlightened, in the Traditional Religions there is a vast selection of names for the gods of the tribes. And having looked very briefly at each of them, it is difficult to see how we can conclude that they are all 'really' the same: just different names for the one God.

All right? All wrong? Only one right?

Quite clearly Allah is not the same as the Christian tri-une God. If Jesus is understood to be only a prophet (even though a highly respected prophet) then he is not the Christian Saviour of the world and most certainly is not the second Person of a Trinity. The same must be true in the case of those Jewish people who reject the assertion that Jesus was their promised Messiah, but a suffering Messiah as foretold by Isaiah, and in fact God incarnate. Krishna has to take his place in a family of deities, quite contrary to the strict monotheism of Islam and Judaism, and to the Christian belief in One God.

The case of the Traditional Religions may well be different. Because the deities of the Traditional Religions are thought of as being far away and uninvolved in the lives of the people they usually have no qualities attached to them. God is the unknown god.

At Athens Paul encountered this unknown god and this is what he said to the Athenians:

> I see that in every way you are very religious. For as I walked around and looked carefully at your objects of worship, I even found an altar with this inscription: TO AN UNKNOWN GOD. Now what you worship as something unknown I am going to proclaim to you (Acts 17:22,23).

Paul was able to identify this god of some, at least, of the Athenians with the God revealed in the Bible and in Jesus, and he could do it precisely because their god had no characteristics to get in the way of the identification. It is precisely by these characteristics that we know who we are talking about: God has revealed himself in the Bible and in Jesus as Creator, as God of love and justice and mercy, but also as Triune. This is a unique revelation. And we are all left with a choice: is this human search for God in vain because there is no God? Are all religions nonsense? Or is it the case that amongst all these religions one is a genuine revelation? What we can't say is that they are really all the same.

Six explanations of religions

There are now and there always have been many religions on offer. There have been at least six different ways of explaining and understanding this surprising fact. The first is the idea of *development*. Religions have been edging closer and closer to the real explanation of our existence. Sir James Frazer produced a massive series of books, *The Golden Bough*[24] which claimed to show this kind of development. But later scholars showed that Frazer had managed to do that by ignoring some aspects of the history of religions that didn't fit his scheme. The second explanation is *relativity*: that each religion is related to a particular culture and fits that culture. There is a measure of truth in this idea: the different *denominations* of Christianity are related to the different *cultures* of their members and religion is always a major part of any people's culture. But if relativity is right then we are left with literally hundreds of religions, all saying different things about this world, about human nature, about how we ought to live.

The third explanation is *secularization*: forget about religion because in the twenty-first century we have moved on from that into a scientific and secular age. Science can't explain everything, but eventually it will be able to, so let's live in the now, rather than bothering about our past and the religions that come from the past. Again there is a problem: the really important questions we ask are 'Why?' questions, and science only answers the 'How?' questions. And another thing: although in the last century it was confidently expected that religion

---

[24] Published in 12 volumes in 1936, this was an attempt to show that religions had developed in a particular way, beginning with an age of magic before religions as such appeared, and with religions becoming steadily more sophisticated. Later critical examination of Frazer's work showed that he had been selective in citing his evidence, omitting bits that didn't fit the thesis, and that no such simple scheme could be justified from the evidence.

would simply wither away like a branch on a dead tree, it hasn't. Religion is alive and flourishing, whether it is Hinduism or Islam or Christianity (in South America, in Africa, in Asia, even if not in Europe).

The fourth explanation is *essence*: in essence they are all the same. The simplest model assumes that Christianity is the true religion. The model looks a little like our solar system, with Christianity at the centre and the other religions circling around it, some closer to it (Judaism and Islam), some further from it (the Traditional Religions, Buddhism). But then it was objected that this model automatically put some religions a long way away from the truth. So a new model emerged with 'The Absolute' at the centre, and then Buddhism and the Traditional Religions could be brought in a little closer to the centre, whatever 'The Absolute' was. But more careful study of the individual religions showed that actually there was no common element in them at all (except, perhaps, the idea that life ought to make sense and doesn't!).

The fifth explanation is *salvation-history*, that God is behind all religions, and has provided a religion for each group of people, a religion that could provide salvation for that group of people and them only. But again it does seem strange that God should give himself the opportunity to produce the world's religions but then produce such a conflicting collection of them. At least they would be expected to have a common core, reflecting the fact that they had a common Author. But they haven't.

The sixth explanation is the common-sense explanation, the *truth-falsehood* explanation, that one of these religions is right and the others wrong. These religions are usually then missionary religions, like Christianity and Islam. Christians and Muslims believe that they have the truth and have the responsibility of sharing the truth with others.

Chapter six

Salvation: The crucial issue

Laws are no help
The two ideas
The eight illustrations
The Holy Spirit

Laws are no help

The universe is anthropic: it is so constructed that human beings can live in one tiny part of it. But too often that tiny part of the universe, our world, is unjust, unfair, filled with suffering and hatred when we feel that it should be filled with love and compassion. Individually we feel ashamed: most of us will admit that we know how we ought to live and what we ought to do, but equally we know that we don't live that way, and don't do what we ought to do. Then there is death: universally feared and yet we all have to go through that door we call death. What is on the other side of it? Something? Nothing? Heaven? Hell?

So we want to escape from ourselves, to escape from what we are and to be something better, to be better in this life, to have a better life on the other side of that door. In fact what we are looking for is a way of salvation. Islam offers a law to be observed and a pathway to follow, the *sunna*, the pathway that was followed by Muhammad. Belief in Allah alone is not enough: salvation, deliverance from one of the seven levels of hell, admission to paradise, depends on following Muham-mad's *sunna*. Once again the problem is that no-one can follow that pathway perfectly: for one thing we don't know what Muhammad did in every part of his life and we have no idea of what he would have done in today's world.

In fact Islam comes up against that simple but brilliant statement of our human problem by Paul:

> I do not understand what I do. For what I want to do I do not do, but what I hate I do . . . I have the desire to do what is good, but I cannot carry it out. For what I do is not the good I want to do; no, the evil I do not want to do – this I keep on doing (Rom. 7:15-19).

Lying behind this peculiar situation is the nature of law: any law seems to create in us a strong objection: 'Why should I?', 'Who's going to make me?' People painting a fence used to put up a notice: 'Wet paint, do not touch!' But they soon found that the commandment was counter-productive: people touched . . . to find out whether the paint really was wet, or just to defy the commandment. So then people who were painting a fence put up a different notice: 'Wet paint! Test here!', and they left a patch of painted fence for people to touch!

To put it theologically (Paul again), 'when the commandment came, sin sprang to life and I died. . . For sin, seizing the opportunity afforded by the commandment, deceived me, and through the commandment put me to death' (Rom. 7:11). It is a strange fact of life that a commandment, especially a prohibition, a 'Thou shalt not!' provokes a revolt. Point out to a child one special book in a bookshelf and say 'No, don't touch!' and at once that book becomes the one thing the child wants. Whether it is the Old Testament Law or Islam's *Shari'a* law, law doesn't save.

The same flaw appears in the very different idea of salvation in Buddhism and Hinduism: behave well and your next life will be better than this life; behave well and you'll attain *nirvana*, you'll escape rebirth into this horrible world, behave well and you'll get to a better world. But what if I don't behave well, or don't behave well enough? Christianity offers a response to those questions: you can't do well enough, you can't obey those laws; what you need is someone who can do for you what you can't do for yourself. In fact you need two Someones. The first Someone is Jesus, who can deal with the sins you *have* committed. The second Someone is the Holy Spirit who can help you not to sin.

The New Testament begins by setting out a very special kind of biography, a 'Gospel'. The gospels aren't regular biographies at all, but concentrate on just three or four crucial years in the life of Jesus, and especially on the last week of his life here. The arrest, the trial, the condemnation, the crucifixion, the burial, the resurrection, the ascension of Jesus are all carefully described, but we are told almost nothing about his childhood or his life as a young man. Then, having described what happened to Jesus, we are quickly introduced to Paul. He was a trained Jewish theologian, and in his letters to the first churches he explained the meaning of what had happened. Jesus was not just a prophet, not just a remarkable teacher, in fact not just a man, but God come to us as a man, come to die for the sins of the world. True, no mere man could have done that: he could only die for his own sins. But an infinite God could take away the infinite sins of the world.

How did Jesus do this amazing thing? Although we can't hope ultimately to understand what Jesus did, still

Paul and others offer us two *ideas* and eight *illustrations* of what has happened.

The two *ideas*

Two over-arching *ideas* set the scene. Firstly, humanity is faced with a losing battle with the Satanic 'Second Kingdom' and needs help in it. Secondly, humanity is in some kind of danger and needs to be saved from it.

There is an immediate problem: while those two problems probably were of importance to the people of Paul's generation, the *ideas* lying behind them are foreign to many people today. Firstly, despite the public proliferation of witches and witches' covens and various expressions of Satanism, few people believe in any representation whatever of Satan or of his supposed kingdom. However, as C.S. Lewis has pointed out, just because we can't believe in the comic figure in red tights and wielding a pitchfork, it does not mean that we can dismiss the Satanic tempter altogether. Secondly, the danger which threatened the sinner with post-death judgment and eternal fire is at least muted and possibly even totally eliminated by the rather general dismissal of such ideas, even by Christians.

Yet the two basic ideas are not so easily dismissed. The losing battle may not appear to be with any Second Kingdom but that does not mean that there is no battle to discuss and no Second Kingdom to be overcome. And we may not be talking about eternal damnation in a literally flaming hell but that does not mean that the fear of death has gone, or that the questioning about death and what happens after it has ended, or that we may blithely assume that after death comes a great nothing, or, alternatively, that somehow after death everyone is welcomed into a beautiful heaven, no matter what their attitude to Jesus and his gospel might have been.

We may somewhat brutally divide humanity into two classes: those who are so engaged with the fight for survival that they have no time for any form of philosophising, and the rest (whether 'the rest' actually give any conscious thought to philosophy or not). For 'the rest' the battle is often the battle with the general meaninglessness of life, epitomised by the cry wrung out of most of us at one time or another, 'It's not fair.' For 'the rest' the danger is that there just might be something beyond death and not mere oblivion; somewhere where the apparent meaninglessness of life will be resolved and where pointed questions will be asked about one's lifestyle.

In this case, salvation is to be seen in terms of someone making sense out of apparent meaninglessness, and bringing justice out of apparent injustice, and someone making an authoritative statement about death and its aftermath, someone who can explain how the comparative mess that I have made of my life can be cleared up so that I don't have to face death with all that on my conscience. Salvation is a crucial matter: dealing with the one great issue that I can do absolutely nothing about: my sin . . . and its eternal consequences.

The eight *illustrations*

The two over-arching *ideas* of salvation and the eight *illustrations* of salvation which follow[25] would all have

---

[25] I am grateful to Professor John McIntyre for the beautifullly clear way in which he has presented the principal terms that have been used in theological discussions on the atonement. See his *The Shape of Soteriology*, Edinburgh, T & T Clark, 1992, chapter 2.

been intelligible and meaningful to the people of Jesus' day, although some would be unfamiliar to some readers today.

The illustration of ransom. In the past, in times of warfare, prisoners were taken but could be *ransomed* by the payment of a price bearing some sort of relationship to the status of the prisoner. In recent years Muslim extremists have kidnapped people and then demanded a ransom for their release.

Jesus is reported as saying that he had come 'not to be served, but to serve, and to give his life as a ransom (*lytron*) for many' (Mt 20:28).

The illustration of redemption. Using a very similar Greek word, we get the illustration of *redemption* (*lytrōsis* and *apolytrōsis*), but here the thought of being released not from someone, a captor, but from something: a habit, a debt, a way of life. Paul writes to the church at Ephesus and says 'In him we have redemption through his blood, the forgiveness of sins, in accordance with the riches of God's grace' (Eph. 1:7).

Then there are two other illustrations which are also related to each other, propitiation (*hilasmos*) and expiation (*hilasterion, hilaskomai*).

The illustration of expiation. Expiation looks at our side of the problem raised by the fact of our sin. We have done wrong. We have to deal with a holy God who demands that we live holy lives. But even if we were able to start doing that right now, we would still have the past sins to deal with. Religions deal with the problem in various ways. Hinduism says that by living a good life in the present I can cancel out at least some of the *karma*, the debt carried forward from my previous life, so that my next life will be better than this one. Islam says that if I leave my *jahiliyya*, my ignorance, acknowledge Allah and his prophet, and follow the *sunna*, the pathway taken by Muhammad, then my good deeds could cancel out at least some of the bad deeds of which I am admittedly guilty.

Judaism generally takes a similar line: obedience to the Law, to *Torah*, is the way to heaven. I recall talking with a Cambridge University undergraduate after I had spoken at a church service about Jesus being the one way to salvation. He asked if that applied to him: he was a Jew. So I asked him: 'Do you believe in heaven?' 'Yes.' 'Do you expect to get there?' 'Yes.' 'How?' 'I must obey the Torah.' 'And do you?' 'No . . . Oh, I see what you mean . . . '

The problem facing these religions is that they have no saviour, no intercessor, to deal with sin, and know that they can't expiate it themselves. Indeed the Qur'an specifically warns that on the day of judgement there will be no intercession allowed (Sura 2: 123). But Christianity takes the problem seriously: some action must be taken so that the relation between us and God can be restored. Just what was done is set out in Paul's letter to the Colossians:

> When you were dead in your sins and in the uncircumcision of your sinful nature,
> i.   God made you alive with Christ.
> ii. He forgave us all our sins,
> iii. having cancelled the written code, with its regulations, that was against us and that stood opposed to us;
> iv. he took it away, nailing it to the cross.
> v.   And having disarmed the powers and authorities, he made a public spectacle of them, triumphing over them by the cross (Col. 2:13-15).

There in those five steps is to be found the expiation offered by Christ, and the comprehensive result of it:

past, present and future all dealt with at the cross. But it is not we who pay the price but Christ: 'Christ Jesus, whom God put forward as an expiation by his blood, to be received by faith' (Rom. 3:24-25, RSV).

The illustration of propitiation. Propitiation might suggest that someone is angry and has to be calmed down, and although a good many theologians have reacted against the thought of God being 'angry', perhaps because of Enlightenment or humanistic or postmodern thinking, still one must ask, why should God *not* be 'angry', at the holocaust, at child abuse . . . or even at absurd human pride? We ourselves consider that it is right for anyone to be angered by such things, and if that is so, then how much more must that be true of a holy God?

We don't have available to us a tidy list of possible sins, with the worst at the top and the unimportant ones at the bottom. Even if we might be tempted to put together that kind of list a little thought would show us that God would not. He is holy and we are not, we would excuse some sins (perhaps because we are guilty of them ourselves) but God would not. Sin is always and everywhere a fist shaken at God, defiance of his laws. As McIntyre puts it, 'Their sin cannot but produce a negative reaction from God if God is to remain all-righteous.'[26]

God is profoundly offended by our sins then, and something has to be done to remove the offence and to restore our relationship with him. The solution is found in the cross.

The illustration of atonement (*katallage*) would at once be familiar to any Jew through the Day of

---

[26] Professor John McIntyre, *The Shape of Soteriology* (Edinburgh: T & T Clark, 1992), p37.

Atonement (*yom kippur*)[27], the annual reminder to the Jewish people both of the sins of the past year and of the manner in which sins were *covered* (*kapar*) through animal sacrifices. The focus here is on the gulf between God, perceived as perfect, sinless, holy, and humanity, epitomised by their continual sinning.

In Hebrews Jesus is presented as High Priest of a new covenant, God incarnate:

> He had to be made like his brothers in every way, in order that he might become a merciful and faithful high priest in service to God, and that he might make atonement for the sins of the people (Heb. 2:17).

The illustration of sacrifice. Atonement is inevitably linked with sacrifice (*thysia*), and the writer of the letter to the Hebrews sees Christ as the fulfilment of the entire Old Testament system of animal sacrifices. But the writer is aware that those sacrifices were being offered as some kind of acknowledgement of sin, but denies that they had any power to deal with sin. But now Christ has offered himself as a sacrifice (Heb. 9:26), perfect in a way that animal sacrifices never could be, and eternal, once for all over against the repeated nature of the sacrifices offered by the Jewish people.

There are just two illustrations remaining, *reconciliation* and *substitution*.

The illustration of reconciliation is very clearly central to 2 Corinthians 5:16-21, where the word itself occurs five times. The text begins with an assertion that for Christians 'everything has become new,' and this is then explained by the fact that they have been reconciled

---

[27] Leviticus 16:11-9 describes the ritual of the annual day of atonement.

to God. So again we have the concept of a barrier between humanity and God, a breakdown of a relationship, and the rift being resolved by Christ. What is important here is the way that reconciliation is expressed. In the Bible it is never God who is reconciled to us, but always we who are reconciled to God. It is not as though God has abandoned us. The problem is that through our surrender to sin we have abandoned God. The problem of restoring the relationship was ours, not God's. However, in an amazing act of grace, the problem is resolved from God's side, not ours. The picture in mind seems to be that of someone in debt who understandably does not wish to meet his creditor, and in any case has no money with which to pay the debt. He then finds that his creditor is offering reconciliation by paying the debt himself.

Being in debt can be a horrible experience. When I was in Ethiopia, a man who lived near me got into debt. His child had died suddenly and tragically. Ethiopian funerals mean that many people come and they all have to be fed, a tent has to be hired for the 'liqso', the weeping. The father of the dead child borrowed ten pounds from the village moneylender. He agreed to pay interest of two pounds a month on the loan. After two years he had paid £240, but still owed ten pounds. I took him to the moneylender and paid the ten pounds, and now he was free of the debt, and at the same time he was reconciled to the moneylender.

Christianity does offer us all a new life, and Paul reminds us

> All this is from God, who reconciled us to himself through Christ and gave us the ministry of reconciliation: that God was reconciling the world to himself in Christ, not counting men's sins against them. And he has

committed to us the message of reconciliation (2 Cor. 5:18-19).

The illustration of substitution. The last illustration to be considered, *substitution*, has its origin in the Old Testament, in Isaiah 53, where the ministry of some unnamed servant of God is being described:

> Surely he took up our infirmities
> and carried our sorrows,
> yet we considered him stricken by God,
> smitten by him, and afflicted.
>
> But he was pierced for our transgressions,
> he was crushed for our iniquities;
> the punishment that brought us peace was upon him,
> and by his wounds we are healed.
>
> We all, like sheep, have gone astray,
> each of us has turned to his own way;
> and the LORD has laid on him
> the iniquity of us all (Is. 53:4-6).

These verses are quoted from the longer passage, Isaiah 52:13-53:12, which is taken to be one of several 'Servant Songs' to be found in Isaiah. The servant in mind is, of course, primarily Israel, or rather that part of Israel that was faithful to God. But through the years of prophetic silence after the time of Malachi, the belief grew amongst the Jewish people that the servant was also to be understood as a coming figure, who would be God's servant to 'save' Israel. Of course there was no thought of that servant being divine. However, Jesus seems to have taken up the idea of the servant and with it the idea of substitution and applied it to himself: 'just as the Son of Man did not come to be served, but to serve' and this is immediately joined to the illustrations both of ransoming and substitution: '. . . and to give his life a ransom for many' (Mt. 20:28).

George Caird, in his book *The Language and Imagery of the Bible*, illustrates and explains this passage from Isaiah beautifully:

> It is as though he had published an advertisement, 'Wanted, a servant of the Lord', accompanied by a job description. He was undoubtedly aware that many famous men, such as Moses and Jeremiah, had sat for the composite portrait he was drawing. What he could not know was that in the end there would be only one applicant for the post.[28]

So we have eight *illustrations* of two basic *ideas* related to the notion of salvation. The *illustrations* of salvation offered by the Bible: ransom, redemption, propitiation, expiation and so on may be relatively unfamiliar to us today, but put together they paint an extraordinary picture of the grand extent of salvation through Christ.

There is another side to the Bible's presentation of the sufferings of Christ which seems to be of particular relevance to people today. The death of Jesus has to be set back in the context of his life, and not isolated from it. Jesus lives a good life, does good, heals, comforts, has compassion. He dares the people to find sin in his life. And yet they crucify him. He shares in the injustice and 'meaninglessness' of life, even to death on a cross, but his resurrection transforms the entire picture. God incarnate comes amongst us, truly man and truly God, lives a

---

[28] G.B. Caird, *The Language and Imagery of the Bible* (London: Duckworth, 1980), p58.

life like that of many of the peasants of his day, but then offers that perfect life as an atoning sacrifice for us all.

The salvation that has been illustrated in eight different ways has three aspects to it: past, present and future. The past can be forgiven. The present can be transformed so that we can live differently, can live 'holy' lives, as disciplined followers of Jesus. As Jesus himself is reported as saying: *You will know them by what they do*. And there is salvation future, the assurance that death is not the end, but a gateway: not a gateway to be feared but rather a gateway to a new and infinitely better life:

> Then I saw a new heaven and a new earth, for the first heaven and the first earth had passed away, and there was no longer any sea. I saw the Holy City, the new Jerusalem, coming down out of heaven from God, prepared as a bride beautifully dressed for her husband. And I heard a loud voice from the throne saying, 'Now the dwelling of God is with men, and he will live with them. They will be his people, and God himself will be with them and be their God. He will wipe every tear from their eyes. There will be no more death or mourning or crying or pain, for the old order of things has passed away' (Rev. 21:1-4).

Of course there is nothing improper in our search for a meaningful theology After all, the theology, which is itself rooted in Jesus who is the grand theme of both Old and New Testaments, explains our faith, shows us how we ought to live, gives us a glimpse into the future. However, precisely how this amazing salvation is brought about remains beyond our finite understanding. It is quite clearly focused on the crucifixion, death and resurrection of Jesus. The eight illustrations all clearly relate to that complex event. But they are illus-trations only, and if any individual illustration is pushed too far, it may become confusing rather than clarifying. Early church theologians such as Origen and Gregory of Nyssa asked if we have been ransomed, to whom was the ransom paid? They came up with some strange answers.[29] But if we find it sometimes difficult to explain how the death and resurrection of Christ sets us free we can demonstrate it powerfully by the quality of life that we now live. And so we come to the Holy Spirit.

The Holy Spirit

The first part of the Christian understanding of salvation is salvation past: dealing with our sin through the death and resurrection of Christ. The second part deals with salvation present, the sending of the Holy Spirit to enable us to live the kind of lives we really want to live. We have to admit that although we are certainly better people than we would have been had we tried to go on living without Jesus, still we are far from perfect. And now comes the truly difficult task: how am I to reconcile the Bible's idealised view of what a Christian is like ('the old has passed away, everything has become new') with the reality seen in the lives of Christians? The fact is that we are 'being changed' and this process is, or perhaps should be, steady and progressive. I rather liked the lapel button which was popular a few years ago. It con-tained just ten capital letters: BPWMGHFWMY, 'Be patient with me; God hasn't finished with me yet.'

The Bible reflects a time when every Christian was a first generation Christian. Christians came to be

---

[29] See McIntyre, *The Shape of Soteriology*, pp30-31.

Christians out of some other religion: Judaism, from which it soon became distinguished, Emperor worship (which usually went alongside some other religion), Greek religion focused on Aphrodite or Asclepius or Artemis. The new allegiance of the Christian was expected to be marked by radically new behaviour. As we have seen, Paul could write in terms of a new creation,[30] the old (presumably the old way of life) having disappeared and the new (again, presumably, the new way of life) having taken its place.

We can get at the nature of this new way of life in two ways: by looking at what was positively expected of Christians and by contrasting that with what was forbidden to Christians. The most comprehensive list of positives and negatives is found in the third chapter of Colossians. Negatively, we have sexual immorality, impurity, lust, evil desires, greed, anger, rage, malice, slander, filthy language and lying. Positively, we have compassion, kindness, humility, gentleness, patience, forbearance, forgiveness and love. Actually there is little here to cause surprise. The sexual excesses clearly reflect the lifestyle of contemporary Greek and Roman society, while the rest of the list is such as any moralist might have produced.

And yet the list is significant in that it majors on conduct, on behaviour that has its source within us rather than on intellectual beliefs or religious practices. There is no mention of any need to make the thrice-yearly visit to the Temple, or even a weekly visit to the synagogue or church, no mention of offering sacrifices, no mention of any particular prayer regime, no reference to fasting. Not that these activities should not have a place in the life of the Christian, but what was significant was the

---

[30] 2 Corinthians 5:17.

outcome of any such practices: prayer and worship and fasting should be reflected in holy living.

The list in Colossians has a second significance: it matches well with the basic idea that salvation implies following Jesus, and following Jesus does mean living in some sense as Jesus did. Not, let it be said, as in the Muslim's attempt to live as Muhammad did, following his dress code and eating habits, but in the much more difficult sense of accepting and applying the morality of Jesus.

So far so good. But how is such a morality to be sustained? There is nothing particularly novel in the morality: other reformers before Jesus had demanded much the same pattern of life from their followers. Experience shows only too well that it is one thing to determine on putting off wrong conduct and putting on new conduct as though they were merely old and new suits which can be changed at will (Colossians uses the imagery of getting undressed and getting dressed in something different), but old habits are not dismissed that easily.

To this problem the New Testament has an answer, the Holy Spirit. Jesus promised his followers that he would provide them with 'another comforter', a *paraclete*, someone who could take his place. This paraclete would help them discern the truth, back up their public testimony, and remind them of what Jesus had said.

There are four references to this 'Counsellor' or 'Comforter', this paraclete, in John's Gospel: John 14:16-18, John 14: 26, John 15:26 and John 16:5-11. Jesus makes it clear to his followers that although he has been with them only for a few years, and must shortly return to his Father, this Comforter will be with them for ever. He is the Spirit of Truth, a truth rejected by the world but accepted by the followers of Jesus. He is the great

teacher: and, especially important for those first disciples, he would remind them of everything that Jesus had
taught them while they were together. So if we ask how
we can be sure that the gospels are reliable, the answer
is because the Holy Spirit reminded the apostles: he was
their memory of those amazing years. The Holy Spirit
would testify to Jesus, not to himself. He is a self-effac-
ing Spirit. And he is the Spirit who backs up, confirms,
what we say when we speak of Jesus:

> He will convict the world of guilt in regard to sin and
> righteousness and judgment: in regard to sin, because
> men do not believe in me; in regard to righteousness,
> because I am going to the Father, where you can see me
> no longer; and in regard to judgment, because the prince
> of this world now stands condemned (Jn. 16:8-11).

Accepting this connection, is it the case that the coming
of this paraclete brings about in Christians a 'new creation'? Preachers not infrequently answer yes, and point
to the transformation of Peter, from a weak, compromis-
ing, denying man into a strong, confident and affirming
man. But that does not do full justice to the evidence.
Peter before Pentecost is intimidated by a woman, Peter
after Pentecost is intimidated by the Christian faction at
Jerusalem which centred on James. Before they arrived
in Antioch Peter went along with Paul's line of teaching
that, as Christians, Jews and Gentiles could eat together
without reference to dietary laws, but after their arrival
he went back to the ideas of James, apparently that
Gentile Christians must observe Jewish laws (Gal.
2:11-21).

But this is a reminder that the work of the Holy Spirit
is progressive, that we aren't suddenly made perfect. We
must remember that Peter *was* different after Pentecost.

See him preaching with power on that same day, so that some three thousand people became Christians (Acts 2:14-41). Or see him only a few days later confidently facing the Jewish rulers who had arrested him and John, and see his courage now: 'Judge for yourselves whether it is right in God's sight to obey you rather than God. For we cannot help speaking about what we have seen and heard' (Acts 4:19-20). In Acts chapter 5 we find Peter and the other apostles being beaten because of their continual preaching about Jesus . . . and '*rejoicing* that they had been counted worthy of suffering disgrace for the Name' (Acts 5:41).

Then there is the example of Paul. Before his famous vision of Jesus he was a persecutor of the Christians and afterwards he becomes an ardent proclaimer of Jesus. There is a radical transformation here. And yet he is far from perfect, having to apologise for his insulting of the Jewish High Priest (Acts 23:3-5) and having so profound a disagreement with Barnabas that the two of them could no longer work together. The public disagreement with Peter at Antioch, recorded in Galatians 2, was, perhaps, not the best way of resolving an important question of theology. But while we may and must accept the fact that we are not perfect, still that should not allow us to be content with what we are. Jesus himself commanded 'Be perfect, therefore, as your heavenly Father is perfect' (Mt. 5:48). Paul told the Christians at Corinth 'Aim for perfection' (2 Cor. 13:11). It is the Holy Spirit who leads us along the road to a perfection that we shall only attain in the Kingdom of heaven.

Despite all the admitted failures of all Christians it is clear that Paul did not expect Christians to go on being the kind of people they were before they became Christians. He describes conversion as a kind of death, and suggests that after that traumatic experience,

Christians should now be living a new kind of life. But Paul was also aware of the danger of the free gift of salvation for people who know that their past is all forgiven and that they are now living 'under grace'. It would be only too easy to ignore that call to perfection, to be satisfied with ourselves as we are, to excuse sin. Indeed, Islam sees this 'under grace' idea as a mere invitation to and some of the very first Christians seem to have taken it that way![31] Paul dismisses that idea pretty vehemently: 'Shall we go on sinning so that grace may increase? By no means! We died to sin' (Rom. 6:1-2)!

The fact is that both the Old Testament and the New Testament are careful to blend together what *might* be, what *ought* to be, and what in reality is.

---

[31] Romans 6:1-14 deals comprehensively with this issue of grace as 'an invitation to sin.'

Chapter seven

Only one God

There can't be two creators
We can't have two sets of rules
Pluralist, inclusivist, exclusivist
How do we know the One God? How can we be sure?
A disappointment:
  The Jews have not recognised their promised Messiah
  The Moslems have not met the real Jesus
'If only you knew' (Jn. 4:10)

There can't be two creators

A good many religions, though not all of them, teach
that it is God who created this universe in which we live.
Scientists now tell us that there may be other universes
but at the moment we know nothing about them so we
don't need to worry about who created them, or
whether they have human beings like us, and whether
those human beings have sinned, like us, and how they
are to be redeemed. But this is our universe, most scientific theories about the universe begin with the idea of a
'big bang' (though they don't have any idea, just yet, of
what caused the big bang), and Christians, Jews and

Muslims believe that it was God who started the whole process. And since we are dealing only with one universe, ours, there can be only one God.

We can't have two sets of rules

But then religions are expected to tell us how we ought to live. Only two centuries ago Hinduism encouraged what was called *thuggee* (from which we get our English word 'thug') which was the ritual killing of any stranger who wandered into Hindu territory. Hinduism also has a caste system (although India's Constitution rejects it), and expects Hindus to marry only within their particular caste. Islam teaches that if Muslims change their religion they are guilty of apostasy for which the punishment is death. Each religion has its own pattern of behaviour, its own ethical system, but they are all different. They don't all say the same thing. To live comfortably each would like to have a system of morality and a matching legal system that is in accord with their beliefs and practices. In Britain there are not a few Muslims who would like to see a second legal system, the Muslim system of Shari'a Law, alongside the one that is now in place. And yet it is difficult to see how we can have two sets of rules for living. How can a country have two sets of laws, without dividing that country into two countries?

It is difficult to find a system for comparing religions, but the Australian scholar Eric Sharpe has suggested that they all contain four elements but in different proportions.[32] Producing a religion, then, is a little like making a

---

[32] Eric Sharpe, *Understanding Religion* (London: Duckworth), 1983, chapter 7.

cake: all sorts of cakes are possible, depending how the ingredients are mixed. Sharpe suggests that every religion has what he calls an *existential* part, the necessity of having individuals who believe that their existence and day-to-day experience depends on their religion. Secondly, there is the *institutional* part of the religion, the way it is organised: do the members meet together and if so, when and how? Are there leaders: if so who are they, what do they do, how are they chosen? Thirdly, there is the *intellectual* part of the religion: some kind of explanation of the origins of the religion and its history. And fourthly there is the ethical aspect of the religion: the part that explains to those who are inside the religion (because there are always people supposed to be outside it) how they ought to live.

This understanding of religions is probably better than trying to divide them into monotheistic and polytheistic and pantheistic religions, since, for example, Muslims would consider Christianity to be polytheistic, and Hindus would consider Hinduism monotheistic. If we use Sharpe's ideas to compare the different Christian denominations we might say that Roman Catholics have more of the institutional in them than the Baptists have, and the Quakers have more ethics than the Anglicans have.

Some Christians worry about the divisions, the denominations, there are within Christianity. However, the diversity is a positive feature (so long as Christians appreciate the differences and accept them), because anyone can find a Christian church which suits their own cultural preferences. If you want more of the institution in your religious cake then maybe the Roman Catholic Church would suit. The fact is that the church's divisions owe far more to culture (the sum total of all that I like to do) than to theology. Some years ago I wrote an article in a Christian newspaper in which I said that few Anglicans know why they are not Methodists and few Brethren know why they are not Baptists. Two weeks later there was an irate letter from a member of the Brethren insisting that most certainly he *did* know why he was not a Baptist, gave ten reasons, and in every one he had misunderstood what Baptists believe.

One of the more heart-warming meetings that I have attended on this whole subject of the differences within Christianity took place in a Baptist church. Representatives were invited from all the other denominations in the district. Then the Baptists were asked to say what they liked about the Anglicans, and the Methodists were asked to say what they admired about the Catholics, and instead of fruitless argument the evening was positive, enlightening and encouraging.

Pluralist, inclusivist, exclusivist

Although there have been many attempts to explain why we have so many religions and why they are all so different, the explanations usually come down to just three: pluralist, inclusivist and exclusivist. What is interesting in this classification is that theologians have recognised that the really vital issue is salvation; not the nature of God or the Trinity or re-incarnation. The pluralists argue that all religions can save, can lead to the One God, and so there is no need for Christian mission. The inclusivists say that the One God is there in all religions, so they can all lead to salvation, but Christianity alone has the real revelation of God, in Jesus. This means that there is a place for mission, but people who are not reached by the message of Christ can still be saved. The exclusivists   maintain   that   religions   other   than

Christianity are human constructions, governed by human ideas, and cannot lead their followers to salvation.

There are two problems lying behind the search for some assessment of the value of the world's religions: the sheer number of religions and their differences and the consequence of the traditional exclusivist idea. If to hear the Good News about Jesus is the only way of salvation, then the vast majority of people who have ever lived on this planet never had any hope of being saved because they never had the chance to hear about Christ. They seem to be lost, because the Jews failed to take their knowledge about God out into the world, and because the Christians took so long to wake up to the need for mission. Did God really create all these myriads of people, knowing that they must ultimately be lost?

The *pluralist position* is best illustrated by John Hick. He rejected the idea that the religions could be seen as a collection of planets, all circling around Christianity. According to this model, Christianity was the centre and it alone was right. The others were more-or-less right depending on how far away they were from Christianity. (There is an interesting observation to be made about this traditional picture: followers of the religions that come nearest to Christianity, Jews and Muslims, prove most resistant to becoming Christians, while followers of religions further away from Christianity, such as the Traditional Religions, have been most ready to move over to Christianity.)

John Hick rejected this model and called for a 'Copernican Revolution'. Just as we had thought of our earth as being the centre of our little bit of the universe, with the sun and the moon circling around it, and Copernicus saw the mistake and put the sun at the centre instead, so Hick took Christianity away from the centre and took it out there amongst the other circling religions. So the religions are all more-or-less right and all more-or-less wrong, and that includes Christianity. And they can all save. Hick based his new model on the principle that God is 'not wanting anyone to perish, but everyone to come to repentance' (2 Pet. 3:9).

This dependence on a Bible text is all very well, but we have to ask, what about the rest of the Bible, the teaching that Jesus is God come in the flesh, dying for the sins of the whole world? The pluralist replies: that is true for Christians and is important for them, but it has no importance at all for those who are in other religions. Similarly, of course, the teaching that Muhammad was the last and final prophet of God is important for Muslims, but not for anyone else.[33]

What we must ask of John Hick is: what is at the centre of your circling religions? At first it was God, but then that left out religions like some forms of Buddhism that don't have God in them. Replacing a personal God with some kind of Absolute failed to resolve the problem. In fact the model itself serves best to illustrate the problem we have seen throughout this book: there is nothing common to all religions, nothing around which they can all circle.

The Inclusivists move away from Hick's ideas in an attempt to find salvation in all religions and yet to insist that Christianity alone has the true revelation of God. The Roman Catholic scholar Karl Rahner produced the notion of 'Anonymous Christianity'. Like Hick, Rahner was troubled by the Bible's clear statement that it is not the will of God that anyone should perish. But then he asked, as Hick had done, how can we explain the fact

---

[33] See Gavin D'Costa, *Theology and Religious Pluralism* (Oxford: Blackwell, 1986), p26.

that most people are not Christians but members of other religions? His answer is that although these other religions are a mixture of truth and error, God is there, by sheer grace, turning sincere members of those religions into anonymous Christians. They don't know that they are really Christians but God's grace makes them so. That they are really Christians is then shown by the fact that God's grace works in them so that they behave as Christians would, showing love and compassion, caring for the poor, giving time to worship and prayer.

The problem here is that it is logical, then, for the Muslim to say that we are all anonymous Muslims and the Hindu that we are all anonymous Hindus.

Thirdly, there is the traditional Christian view, exclusivism. This view, which states that salvation comes to us through Christ and only through Christ, is a view that takes the Bible seriously. John Hick saw the Bible as a collection of myths. The incarnation was to be taken as a myth, not as history. Exclusivists insist that Christianity is unique among the religions because in it and in it alone God has fully revealed himself. Salvation comes through Christ and only through Christ.

Most Christians modify this exclusivism. First of all they point out that babies and small children die long before they could possibly understand the Good News, and so God's grace saves them, but still it is on the basis of the death and resurrection of Jesus. The same is then true for people who have mental problems, and couldn't understand the Gospel. But then what about all those millions who have never heard of Christ? To answer this question we have the difference between what is called *special revelation*, the unique, wonderful, special revelation of who God is that came through Jesus, and *general revelation*, nature, which reveals God's power. Paul wrote:

> Since the creation of the world God's invisible qualities
> – his eternal power and divine nature – have been
> clearly seen, being understood from what has been
> made (Rom. 1:20).

Paul goes on to explain that it is those who have seen all
that eternal power in creation, and have rejected it and
worshipped the things that have been created instead of
the One God who created them, who are condemned.

Speaking to a crowd of philosophers in Athens Paul
said:

> From one man he made every nation of men, that they
> should inhabit the whole earth; and he determined the
> times set for them and the exact places where they
> should live. God did this so that men would seek him
> and perhaps reach out for him and find him, though he
> is not far from each one of us (Acts 17:26-27).

So Paul suggests that in designing this *anthropic* universe, this universe so designed that we would eventually appear in some corner of it, God went further: he so
designed this corner that it would cause people to see
God through it, to find him because of it.

Paul's view reflects an even more positive view of
people throughout the world who have received no special revelation and have had to depend on general revelation: no prophets, no Law, no Bible, just the evidence
of the world they could see around them. The prophet
Malachi was profoundly dismissive of the religiosity of
the Jewish people of his day:

> "So I will come near to you for judgment. I will be quick
> to testify against sorcerers, adulterers and perjurers,
> against those who defraud labourers of their wages, who

oppress the widows and the fatherless, and deprive aliens of justice, but do not fear me," says the LORD Almighty (Mal. 3:5).

In astonishing contrast, says Malachi, people without all the advantages the Jews had did fear God:

> "My name is great among the nations, from the rising to the setting of the sun. In every place incense and pure offerings will be brought to my name, because my name (is) great among the nations," says the LORD Almighty (Mal. 1:11).

This is so astonishing that the NIV translation has 'will be great' instead of 'is great', (that change can be made because the Hebrew of this verse doesn't have a verb 'is' or 'will be' in it). But it is quite obvious that Malachi is contrasting what the Jews were doing, despising God, and what the rest of the world was doing, honouring God. Without special revelation, many people had found God in creation, had realised how great he must be, and were honouring him and even worshipping him.

How do we know the One God? How can we be sure?

Abraham claimed that Yahweh spoke to him, Moses claimed that Yahweh actually appeared to him. Muhammad said that while in the cave Hira just outside Mecca, Gabriel, the messenger of Allah, appeared to him. Gautama the Buddha is said to have gained enlightenment, an understanding of the fundamental truth about life, while sitting under a fig tree. Karl Marx was sitting in the Reading Room of the British Museum when he thought that he had found the rules that govern society.

Christianity is different: it claims that God himself came here to us: not a prophet, not a priest but God himself, coming into time from eternity. So here was the ultimate revelation: God himself telling us how we ought to live and what we ought to do: not God passing on a message through some human leader who would inevitably be quite capable of getting it wrong.

In fact there are two crucial events in this incarnation: the virgin birth of Jesus at one end and the resurrection-ascension at the other end. Even the Qur'an admits that Jesus was born of Mary, who was a virgin. But amongst Christians there has been argument: Bishop David Jenkins, former Bishop of Durham did not believe in the virgin birth, although he admitted that God could have arranged a virgin birth. But the Bible evidence is quite clear.

In the prophecy in Isaiah that promises that 'a virgin shall conceive and bear a child' the Hebrew word that is translated 'virgin' means no more than a young woman, who might or might not be a virgin. It is also true that the prophecy originally was meant as a sign to Israel that they would very soon be delivered from the attack of the northern kingdom and the Syrians. It may even be that the promised sign of a child born to a young woman was Isaiah's own son, Maher-Shalal-Hash-Baz (Is. 8:1). But prophecies might be fulfilled two or even more times, as in this case, once near to the time when the prophecy was given and again at some much later time.

More importantly, however, where the Isaiah prophecy is mentioned in the New Testament (Mt. 1:23) the Greek word used *does* mean 'virgin', and Matthew saw the Isaiah prophecy as referring both to a young woman (not a virgin) of Isaiah's day *and* a young woman, Mary, a virgin.

But the virgin birth of Jesus is not only the fulfilment of an ancient prophecy, nor is it merely a miracle, a sign. Nor is it intended to be a guarantee that Jesus would be free of 'original sin', a sinful nature inherited from human parents, for if that were the case not only would Mary have to be free from sin, but so would her parents . . . and so on right back to the beginnings of the human race. The virgin birth is the guarantee that Jesus is not summoned into the world by any human action, by any sex act, but solely by the free decision of God, when the time was right. As Paul later put it in his letter to the Galatian Christians:

> When the time had fully come, God sent his Son, born of a woman, born under law, to redeem those under the law, that we might receive the full rights of sons (Gal. 4:4,5).

At the other end of his life we have the resurrection of Jesus. This is absolutely crucial to any understanding of who Jesus is. It seems that on several occasions Jesus had told his followers that he would be killed, but that he would rise again. In some sense anyone could have taught what Jesus taught, and even his miracles didn't make him anything more than human: Moses, Elijah, Elisha, Paul, Peter, were all credited with miracles. The death of Jesus was the great test of his claim to being one with the Father.

When the apostles came to preach Jesus, what they emphasised was the resurrection. It wasn't at all difficult to show that Jesus was crucified, but what was really new was the resurrection. So Paul pointed out the great number of people who had seen Jesus *after* his crucifixion, including five hundred people at one time. And, wrote Paul, defiantly, 'most of them are still alive'. . . so ask them (1 Cor. 15:6)!

These two unique events mark out Jesus as unique, unlike the rest of the millions of human beings who have ever lived out their lives here. On the one hand he was truly human, growing up as a child, being obedient to Mary and Joseph, collecting together a few followers, teaching, eating, drinking, getting tired, sleeping. On the other hand, he was born of a virgin, but crucified, risen, ascended, glorified.

A disappointment

The Jews have not recognised their promised Messiah
The Muslims have not met the real Jesus

Every generation has to discover the real Jesus. That's not easy, because he is hidden in so much ritual, so much gobbledygook, so many institutions, so many theologies. Just occasionally we encounter him, perhaps unexpectedly, in an unexpected place or in an unexpected person.

I met him in Sister Gabriel. We both lived and worked in Ethiopia. We both had a deep concern for the poor. At the time when I met her she was working amongst the burnt-out leprosy cases. They lived amongst the graves in the churchyards of the Addis Ababa Orthodox churches. Someone said to me, 'Peter, you ought to meet Sister Gabriel.' But she was a Roman Catholic. I was a Protestant, in an ultra-Protestant missionary society which scarcely recognised Catholics as being Christians at all. And yet . . . I agreed to meet her. And I still remember as she walked towards me, her hand outstretched (and the twinkle in her eye which told me that she knew all about my hesitations and doubts) we were at one: we both loved Jesus, and she, at least, was living the Jesus way. She was then in her seventies: she introduced me to a young Catholic priest who worked with her. 'This', she said, with that twinkle even more pronounced, 'this is *Father* Robert.' I couldn't help laughing at the absurdity: this spiritually mature elderly, serene Christian lady and the young, uncertain, untried 'Father' Robert. Years later, when she was in her eighties, I read that she was still at work in Ethiopia amongst the famine victims in the north.

One Christian I would like to have met was Harold St John. One story about him caught my attention. He was travelling on a rather packed London Underground train. He looked along the carriage and saw a man he had never seen before. He edged along until they could talk, and said, 'Excuse me, I think you know a Friend of mine.' And the man replied, 'Yes, I love Jesus too'! There was something on the faces of both of them that reflected Jesus, and each of them could see it in the other.

But sadly, despite the insistence of the first Christians that Jesus was the anointed one, the Messiah they were looking for, despite the fact that almost all of the first Christians were Jews, in the main the Jewish people have rejected Jesus. The Orthodox amongst them continue to expect the Messiah, while others have quietly set aside any Messianic expectations.

We have been quick to apologise to the Muslim world for what so-called Christians did in the Crusades, although we have been less ready to own up to our mistreatment of the Jews. Once Christianity became politically powerful, adopted by the Roman Emperor Constantine, Christians began to flex their muscles. Jews were actually banned from Jerusalem. Later on Jews were required to wear distinctive dress (a nasty foreshadowing of the Nazi persecution of the Jews who were forced to wear the Star of David to mark them out from Aryan Germans). The so-called Muslim Covenant of Umar, which set out the restrictions to be placed by Muslims on Jews and Christians, was probably based on a similar Covenant produced by the Christian Emperor Justinian I in 534AD, the Justinian Codex.

More forcibly for today, the Jews find it difficult to forget or forgive the Nazi persecution that led to the death of millions of Jews. It is generally true that, with a few honourable exceptions, the Christian Church in Germany did little to protest about what was being done.

It seems that too often there is a difference between the face of the Church and the face of our all-too-few Sister Gabriels.

The world of Islam has fared no better than the Jewish people in encountering the real Jesus. The Qur'an does not contain a description of any of his miracles, although it does admit that he healed the sick and raised the dead, and none of his parables are given. In fact Jesus is reduced to a highly respected prophet. Most significantly, of course, the Qur'an denies that Jesus was God incarnate, and denies that he was crucified.

Ever since the rise of Islam, history has very largely been a history of the clash between Christian empires and successive Muslim empires. Undoubtedly the most significant clash has been over Jerusalem, the city that has special significance for Jews, Muslims and Christians. The Crusades were sparked off by increasing attacks on Christian pilgrims trying to visit Jerusalem. Already, thirty years before the first Crusade, seven thousand German pilgrims had been attacked by Muslims. The Christians were virtually defenceless as they had depended on their sacred role as pilgrims for protection. In 1096 Christian patience at last ran out and

Pope Urban II encouraged the first Crusade. Three years later the Crusaders captured Jerusalem. The scene was horrendous: men, women and children were slaughtered. The Jews took refuge in the main synagogue but the Crusaders set it on fire, and they were burned to death. One writer says that in Jerusalem that day 'blood ran ankle deep.' In all this carnage there was no sign of the love of Jesus. And yet despite the fact that it all happened more than nine hundred years ago, many Muslims still see it as typical of Christianity.

Perhaps it is as well to remember that in the midst of the hatred and bloodshed stirred up by the Crusades, the Christian missionary Francis of Assisi went to Egypt during the Fifth Crusade in 1219, not to fight but to talk about Jesus. According to one of his friends he hoped to put an end to the Crusades by converting both sides! Apparently he was courteously received even by the Sultan, al-Malik al-Kamil, and some (probably over-optimistic) reports suggested that the Sultan became a closet Christian. We do know that just after his meeting with St Francis, the Sultan ordered the release of some 30,000 Christian prisoners, and commanded that they should be treated with respect.[34] Sadly it is the fighting of the Crusaders that is remembered today, and the pleading of the missionary is forgotten.

'If only you knew' (Jn. 4:10)

In all the confusion of Christian denominations and systematic theologies, and councils and committees and assemblies, it is only too easy to lose sight of Jesus. In

---

[34] See Christine Mallouhis's book, *Waging Peace on Islam* (London: Monarch, 2000), chapter 8.

chapter four of John's Gospel we find Jesus sitting by himself near to a well. His students have gone off to a nearby village to buy something to eat. It was hot, midday, Jesus was tired. And then something surprising happens: a woman comes to draw water. It was certainly surprising for her: she had not expected to find anyone at the well: midday was not at all the usual time for women to fetch water, and men don't carry water so they aren't usually found at the well. It was not merely surprising: it was embarrassing. Embarrassing firstly because the woman didn't expect to find anyone there at the well, secondly because a man and a woman who were strangers wouldn't meet unless there were other people around, and thirdly because the woman was not a Jew, but a Samaritan, and Jews and Samaritans simply didn't mix. There was another problem which the woman thought wouldn't arise: she had been married five times, and was not married to the man she was then living with. That was why she was at the well at midday, hoping to avoid the critical stares and rough remarks of the other women.

She did her best simply to ignore this stranger. She let down the bucket on its rope and drew up the bucket brimming with cool water. 'Will you give me a drink?' The voice was a shock. They had met accidentally, but at least propriety demanded that they should not speak. She objected: 'You are a Jew and I am a Samaritan woman. How can you ask me for a drink?' The reply of Jesus could be the reply of Jesus to Jews and Muslims and Hindus and Sikhs around the world today: 'If you knew who it is . . . ' She didn't know who he was. A man, a Jew, certainly a very unconventional man, since he spoke to her. Very shortly, when she discovered that he knew all about her marital adventures, she would admit that he was a prophet. But still, 'If you knew . . . ' In today's western world where we are so proud of our achievements: our refrigerators, our cars, our trains, our flights to the ends of the earth, our supersonic aircraft, our space shuttles, our familiarity with one another, it is only too easy to be overly familiar with Jesus, because we don't really know who he is. If we did, the use of his name in thoughtless swearing would stop. The woman at the well simply had no idea of who it was who was speaking to her. She, a speck in the universe, created through the tired Man who sat there near the well, she, with all her mixed-up life, she was talking with God enfleshed.

She was talking easily, comfortably, with the one who has revealed the One God to us, who could say 'Anyone who has seen me has seen the Father', and 'I and my Father are One.' He was a great teacher: as the people who heard him said, he taught like someone who had authority. He had amazing power, even over nature: 'What kind of man is this? Even the winds and the waves obey him.' He could heal people, cure them of the much feared leprosy, even bring the dead back to life. But, far more importantly, he was the One God come to us, come near to us. John puts this vital fact at the beginning of his gospel, and again at the end:

> In the beginning was the Word, and the Word was with God, and the Word was God (Jn. 1:1).

Doubting Thomas, who had missed the appearance of the Risen Jesus to the other ten disciples, and who simply would not believe that Jesus was risen, was confronted by him just one week after that other appearance. His doubts disappeared:

'My Lord and my God.'